The RETIREMENT BIBLE

Learn Strategies to Successfully manage your money decisions for the rest of your life.

STEPHEN LOMSDALEN

The Retirement Bible: Learn Strategies to Successfully Manage your money decisions for the rest of your life.
Stephen Lomsdalen © 2014

Securities and Investment Advisory services offered through Brokers International Financial Services, LLC, Panora, IA, Member FINRA/SIPC

Interior Design: Fusion Creative Works, fusioncw.com
Cover Design: The NETMEN CORP
Editor/Proofreader: Beverly Holloran
Special thanks to Richard Best and www.christianpf.com

ISBN: 978-1-497310-57-5

Published by:

TANDEM
HOUSE

Printed in the United States of America

Contents

INTRODUCTION

As anyone would have expected, the extraordinary convergence of extreme stock market volatility, low interest rates, declining home values, diminished retirement savings accounts, chronic unemployment, and the irresponsible fiscal management of our government has taken a severe toll on the American psyche. The 2012 Employee Benefit Research Institute (EBRI) Retirement Confidence Survey finds that Americans' confidence in their ability to afford a comfortable retirement continues to slide. The EBRI states that this slide may be in fact contributed toward more immediate financial concerns about job uncertainty, debt, and financial security. At the same time, the percentage of Americans saving for retirement continues its gradual decline.

Many people remain uncomfortable making even basic decisions about money. A majority of Americans appear to be frozen in fear as a crisis of confidence tightens its grip on their psyche. The correlation between confidence and outcome is unmistakable. Absent confidence in their ability to save enough for retirement, many people turn their attention to other concerns or simply escape their worries by living in the here and now. Between the growing uncertainty of the financial markets and the increasing complexity of planning for long-term needs, people have lost their ability to think strategically about their future.

In this digital age of the Internet, 24/7 cable news, instant communications, and social media, you might think that the average person would gain many of the advantages of knowledge and insight once only enjoyed by the financial services industry. There is no shortage of free investment advice; which streams non-stop over the cable channels and through hundreds of investment websites. And, if it is professional advice you are seeking, you can choose from among the 300,000 plus financial professionals who populate hundreds of banks, brokerage firms, independent broker-dealers, and insurance companies across the land.

Advantages? There are no advantages in information overload; at best, it creates confusion and paralysis by analysis. Considering that most of these information sources exist in order to sell advertising, there is little to gain from tips and advice that do not reflect your personal needs and values. Yes, it is possible to glean some worthwhile information and unquestionably it pays to stay informed, but for the average person, it is nearly impossible to filter out information that can be of use.

Unfortunately, access to more information and technology has not improved the financial picture for most people over the last couple of decades. Instead of providing more clarity, it is now more difficult to discern between fact and fiction. People without the knowledge and experience, or the proper frame of reference can just as easily adopt the myth as they can the reality. It is only through their unfortunate experiences that they realize their mistakes.

While I'm not suggesting that you should turn off your cable news or refrain from surfing investment sites, you do need to remind yourself that these sources of information don't necessarily share your values or agenda. Gathering information and educating yourself are essential parts of the process; it should be done in the context of your clearly defined goals, along with a well-conceived financial plan grounded in proven financial principles.

FINANCIAL PRINCIPLES STEEPED IN WISDOM

For more than two millenniums, people have been turning to the Bible to search for answers and guidance in all aspects of their lives. Yet, it still surprises most people to learn there are hundreds of verses in the Bible about money matters. More than half of the parables Jesus used in His teachings deal specifically with finances. In fact, it could be said that the Bible was the first financial planning guide, replete with basic principles that govern every aspect of our financial lives.

While the books of the Bible may be thousands of years old, the financial principles espoused within their pages are as valid today as they have ever been. As Solomon said, "There is nothing new under the sun." Very little differentiates the financial concerns between the people of the Biblical era and people of today. Some may say that the methods for dealing with them have changed. Even today, after you strip all of the technology and financial theories (those Biblical principles) handed down through hundreds of years of teachings, are timeless in their application.

Take, for example, a study conducted in 2010 by the University of Colorado to determine that true happiness cannot be found with money alone. This is not exactly ground-breaking when you consider that the book of Ecclesiastes said precisely the same thing:

He who loves money will not be satisfied with money, nor he who loves abundance with its income. This too is vanity. [Ecclesiastes 5:10]

The study also found that if your pursuit of happiness is driven by materialism, you will not only be less happy than other people, you will be liked by less people as well. Better to pursue happiness through life experiences and other people, than to covet money and material goods. It seems that a study costing hundreds of thousands of dollars is required to match the wisdom of God.

The real practical value of Biblical wisdom is that it is transcends time and circumstances. Regardless of the economic environment, tax laws, which political party is in power, or the latest technology, Biblical wisdom doesn't need to change. No matter your age, income, or financial circumstances, it remains steadfastly true and useful. Considering its simplicity and its universal application across regions and generations, it's truly a wonder why more people don't turn to it for their financial guidance before they get into financial trouble.

"Therefore everyone who hears these words of Mine and acts on them, may be compared to a wise man who built his house on the rock. And the rain fell, and the floods came, and the winds blew and slammed against that house; and yet it did not fall, for it had been founded on the rock. Everyone who hears these words of Mine and does not act on them, will be like a foolish man who built his house on the sand. The rain fell, and the floods came, and the winds blew and slammed against that house; and it fell—and great was its fall." [Matthew 7:24-27]

At the core of God's Word for financial advice are key principles centered on achieving financial freedom. This is perhaps not the "financial freedom" most people think of along the lines of "financial independence;" rather, it's freedom from the bondage that can enslave us if we don't follow the principles. Where you go from there – whether it's to accumulate as much wealth as you can or want, or to simply fulfill your ambition of a good life – these principles are the bedrock that enables you to overcome the obstacles to pursuing your financial independence.

Depending on one's interpretation of the many books of the Bible that address issues of money, one could easily glean as many as ten or fifteen overriding principles that can guide our financial lives. To simplify and clarify, I've culled five principles that, if strictly followed, can put you squarely on the path to financial freedom.

PRINCIPLE #1: LIVE WITHIN YOUR MEANS

There is precious treasure and oil in the dwelling of the wise, but a foolish man swallows it up. [Proverbs 21:20]

For many unfortunate Americans it took a crippling financial crisis to awaken them to the reality that spending more than they earn can have devastating consequences. In this age of easy credit and the irrational pursuit of more, too many people now find themselves struggling in bondage. The primary difference between them and those who emerged from the crisis unscathed or even thriving, is that the latter have the self-discipline to live at or below their means.

It all comes down to lifestyle choices we make each day to determine the incremental changes that will lead us to financial freedom or bondage. Going one step farther by avoiding indulgences and living beneath our means enables us to build the financial margin essential for peace of mind and ultimate financial success.

PRINCIPLE #2: LIVE DEBT-FREE

The rich rules over the poor, and the borrower becomes the lender's slave. [Proverbs 22:7]

We only need to look back a few years to understand the tragic consequences that debt can have in the lives of people who can't control it. Even a small amount of debt can interfere with our freedom to pursue our life's course. We can only serve one master, and, if our servitude is hijacked by our creditors, we cannot be financially or spiritually free to serve the Lord in the way that He asks of us.

PRINCIPLE #3: BUILD RESERVES

Go to the ant, O sluggard, observe her ways and be wise, which, having no chief, officer or ruler, prepares her food in the summer and gathers her provision in the harvest. [Proverbs 6:6-8]

Creating sufficient savings and investments are essential to prepare for the uncertainties of life and achieving financial independence. The Bible teaches us that, while this is important, we shouldn't make the accumulation of wealth our ultimate financial goal in life. Sufficiency, that which can sustain our idea of a good life for the rest of our lives, should be the goal, lest we develop an unhealthy attachment to money. When it comes to money, the pursuit of more never leads to happiness because, if that is the goal, we can never be satisfied.

PRINCIPLE #4: ESTABLISH LONG-TERM GOALS

The mind of man plans his way, but the LORD directs his steps. [Proverbs 16:9]

The first three principles are the means to the end of achieving the goals you establish for yourself. Living within your means to create the financial margin that allows you to avoid debt and build a reserve is vital in order to live financially free; but it's your long-term goals that will guide you in your long-term investment decisions.

PRINCIPLE #5: SEEK FINANCIAL COUNSEL

He who walks with wise men will be wise, but the companion of fools will suffer harm. [Proverbs 13:20]

As simple as these principles are to understand, following them has been made difficult by the increasing complexity of our financial world. The myriad tax laws, financial products, and competing financial advice, all filtered through the noise of constant media and advertising barrages; make it nearly impossible for anyone to make the right decisions with any degree of confidence. The counsel of an objective, conflict-free financial advisor can be invaluable for narrowing your choices and finding the right path to your financial independence.

Selecting the right financial advisor is one of the most important decisions you can make. While there are specific criteria that should be used (see Chapter 15), the most important is that your advisor shares your beliefs and values.

IF YOU CAN'T TAKE IT WITH YOU— DOES IT REALLY BELONG TO YOU?

For we have brought nothing into the world, so we cannot take anything out of it either. [1 Timothy 6:7]

For me, these key principles that surface from the hundreds of verses throughout the Bible tell us that sound financial advice has always been at the core of living a fulfilling life. It is important to note, however, that these principles emanate from a single, overriding tenet that gives them their validity; and that is that *God owns everything*.

What exactly does that mean? Even the most faithful Christians might wonder why, if they earned their money with their knowledge, skills and abilities, it should all belong to God. The Bible poses that it is God who gives us the knowledge, skills and abilities to earn that money, and, therefore, gives us the power to create wealth; so shouldn't it belong to Him? Following that logic then, we are merely stewards of His wealth, tasked with managing it effectively to further His work here on earth.

So, for those of us who believe that our 10 percent tithe is all that belongs to God, in His eyes we have been chosen to be the stewards to effectively manage the other 90 percent of His resources according to His principles and standards.

If you're among the many who are asking, "What's in it for me?" that's a perfectly valid question and one that the Bible answers in numerous ways:

'For I know the plans that I have for you,' declares the LORD, *'plans for welfare and not for calamity to give you a future and a hope.'* [Jeremiah 29:11]

If we are indeed God's children, we should expect that He does have plans for each of us; and if we learn from His wisdom and follow His directives, it stands to reason that we should benefit from His plans.

His master said to him, 'Well done, good and faithful slave. You were faithful with a few things, I will put you in charge of many things; enter into the joy of your master.' [Matthew 25:23]

As the above verse says, "*You were faithful with a few things, I will put you in charge of many things.*" Our only responsibility then is to accept God's priorities for us and manage what He has provided to demonstrate we are worthy of managing more. In doing so, the burden of providing our needs and realizing prosperity falls to Him.

Accepting God's priorities in our lives does not have to mean that we become a minister or drop everything to trek off to a third-world country to rescue the suffering. What it does mean is, perhaps, to spend our time being the best parent, boss, or employee we can be by being kind hearted, just, fair, and devout in our dealings with those around us. Spending a little more time with the Word or seeking God's wisdom through prayer would go a long way as well.

What the Bible teaches us is that there are really just two paths in life: that which the foolish follow, or the way of the wise. We have the distinct choice of following the way of the foolish by trying to do things on our own and enduring the long and painful experience of trial and error; or we can acquire the wisdom that comes from His Word and seek the counsel of the wise.

THE WISDOM TO SAVE US FROM OURSELVES

By wisdom a house is built, and by understanding it is established; and by knowledge the rooms are filled with all precious and pleasant riches. [Proverbs 24:3-4]

One of the biggest misconceptions about the Bible's teachings is the notion that money, or having money is bad. But a closer study of its words helps us understand that it isn't money that is bad; it's the misuse of it that is at the root of evil. It really comes down to your attitude about money: whether you are vulnerable to the tools of evil as they are manifested in greed, ego, vanity and pride. These are the very emotions that God warns us to guard against lest they control our financial lives.

In the management of money, our chief problem and even our worst enemy is often ourselves, especially when we allow ourselves to act without any guiding principles or strict adherence to time tested practices. The financial principles of the Bible, and all of the wisdom contained within its pages, provide a blueprint for financial management. This enables us to shield our financial decisions from our emotions to ensure that we manage His resources according to His plan. Specifically, it ensures that you can manage your money more effectively according to the plan He placed in your heart using the steps He provides.

In the chapters that follow, I will break the five Biblical principles down into the many aspects of our financial lives in order to focus on God's wisdom as it applies to each. Within each chapter, you will uncover specific practices that, when implemented, will help you fend off the financial bondage that prevents so many people from achieving their ambition of a good life.

I encourage you to use this book, not only as a way to better understand your relationship with God in the financial sense, but also as a practical guide on your path to financial freedom and, ultimately, financial independence.

Chapter One

BUDGETING

Over the last few decades, many Americans have deceived themselves into believing that the markets, along with their incomes, will always continue to rise; providing the rationale for their paycheck-to-paycheck style of living. According to the 2012 National Financial Capability Study conducted by the Financial Industry National Regulatory Authority Education Foundation, fewer than half (41 percent) of Americans surveyed reported spending less than their income, and more than half (56 percent) don't have any rainy day savings to cover three months of unanticipated financial emergencies.[1] Many have learned the hard way that the markets don't always go up and incomes are never secure. In fact, incomes have shrunk over the last decade. And, of course, nearly twenty million people have lost all or a part of their incomes altogether due to the down economy.[2]

The problems for many people are compounded by their relentless pursuit of more, which is enabled by the availability of easy credit. In 2013, the average consumer debt held by

---

1 The 2012 National Financial Capability Study conducted by the FINRA Education Foundation. http://www.usfinancialcapability.org

2 US Department of Labor, Bureau of Labor Statistics. Employment Situation Summary. July 2013. (11.2 million unemployed as of July 2013, and 8.5 million involuntary part-time workers.)

American households exceeds $22,000.[3] In today's hyper commercial world, we have been conditioned throughout our lives to strive ever upward in pursuit of more. It's the sole objective of advertisers to make us believe that our lives will be better if we own their product(s).

And, as is typical in our western culture, many people measure their own lifestyle by comparing it with others, rather than criteria rooted in personal beliefs and values. In the pursuit of more, we lose sight of what we have, which is really the only proof of what we can reasonably expect to produce, both now and in the future. The failure to appreciate the lifestyle we have increases the "risk of more" with absolutely no guarantee of increased happiness.

When we allow ourselves to confuse our discontent over current lifestyle with a clear ambition of achieving what we deem to be a good life, we will probably resist making the difficult choices to secure our financial future. If we are not content with the life we have, we are not likely to be content, even when we get more. So the pursuit of more will continue at the expense of the actions needed now to achieve a lifetime of sufficiency.

THE VIRTUE OF DILIGENCE

Know well the condition of your flocks, and pay attention to your herds. [Proverbs 27:23]

From Biblical times through to the present day, a farmer's flocks have always represented his wealth. To know the condition of your flocks, or, in today's terms, your financial assets,

---

3 Federal Reserve G-19 Consumer Credit Report. January 2013. (As of January 2013, Americans held $850.9 billion in credit card debt or $6,920 per household; $1.944 trillion in school, auto, furniture loans, or $15,800 per household.)

is to know where you stand in your ability to meet your family's needs. It means being diligent in assessing your financial means, your current financial condition, and your financial outlook to know if you are living within your means.

It's nearly impossible to consistently produce the essential financial margin for building reserves if you aren't aware of what's coming in versus what's going out. More important, should your flock become diseased or sick (job loss, unexpected expenses, disability, etc.), how will you provide for your family?

Beyond that, are you *paying attention to your herds?* There is a big difference between knowing the condition of your flocks and attending to the *needs of your herds* – otherwise referred to as the *concerns and needs of your family.* You may be able to pay the bills today and even indulge in some extravagances for your family; but what about their needs tomorrow or in the years ahead? Will you be caught off guard when the unexpected occurs? Are your own pursuits consistent with the care of your family in the present and future?

No matter where you stand financially, a wise person is always diligent in knowing the condition of his finances and attending to the present and future needs of his family...

> *For riches are not forever, nor does a crown endure to all generations.* [Proverbs 27:24]

BE PREPARED

The overwhelming number of Bible verses speaking to the need to prepare for the unexpected tells us that the failure to do so was as prevalent then as it is today. And, the consequences were no less painful.

Go to the ant, O sluggard, observe her ways and be wise, which, having no chief, officer or ruler, prepares her food in the summer and gathers her provision in the harvest. [Proverbs 6:6-8]

Unexpected expenses and events are to be expected, so planning for them is simply the wise course to take, no matter your financial situation. Establishing an emergency reserve of six to twelve months of living expenses is not only prudent, it's the responsible thing to do. Between job losses, disabilities, major repairs, and medical or family emergencies, there is a likely chance that we each will experience an interruption of our income or a major unplanned expense.

ESTABLISH A SPENDING PLAN

On the first day of every week each one of you is to put aside and save, as he may prosper, so that no collections be made when I come. [1 Corinthians 16:2]

At the core of any successful financial enterprise, be it a household or a business, is a sound and effective budget plan that is used to drive all spending decisions, large and small, on a daily basis. Businesses have profit goals and families have savings goals. Both types of goals require budgeting and cash flow management to meet them consistently. Using the tools that are available to you online and in software packages will give you the ability to budget like a pro and manage your surpluses to increase your giving and your savings.

Your spending plan should be developed around your essential expenses, such as housing, food, transportation, etc., as priorities. Next, it's important to set a monthly goal for giving and for saving, and then plan your nonessential expenses (entertainment, dining out, purchases, etc.) around this goal.

If you also have a debt reduction goal, a portion of your surplus should go toward paying off the debt, but, ideally, not at the expense of your giving or savings. This should be over and above your regular monthly debt payments. Find a balance between the two and divide your payment to yourself between your obligations (ie: 10 percent to giving, 60 percent to savings, and 40 percent to debt reduction). The important thing is to maintain the balance and stick with it each month. As your debt decreases you can then apply more to savings.

The key to successful budgeting is maintaining the discipline to keep your expenses in line. If you exceed a planned expenditure one month, you should find another one to cut in order to achieve your spending goal.

AVOID TEMPTATION

Like a city that is broken into and without walls is a man who has no control over his spirit. [Proverbs 25:28]

We all have succumbed to the impulse to buy at one time or another, but some people lack the will or desire to control their impulses. It is probably the single biggest reason why people go in to debt. If you can live without it, you don't need to buy it – certainly not if it means going into debt.

PLAN AHEAD

> *For which one of you, when he wants to build a tower, does not first sit down and calculate the cost to see if he has enough to complete it? Otherwise, when he has laid a foundation and is not able to finish, all who observe it begin to ridicule him, saying, 'This man began to build and was not able to finish.'*
> [Luke 14:28-30]

Here Jesus is speaking to His disciples about the costs they must bear in order to follow Him. The answer many people might give today is likely to be "no," because they can simply put it on their credit card. Future planned expenses, such as vacations, should be budgeted ahead of time with sufficient savings set aside each month in order to avoid incurring additional debt. Major purchases, unless they are required immediately, should also be planned in advance.

Summary

Developing and adhering to a strict spending plan is the core strategy for following Principle #1: Live Within Your Means. It all comes down to lifestyle choices we make each day: developing good habits, and acquiring the critical ability to just say "no." But this has to start with an action plan to get your spending under control. Like most people, the sacrifices you must make will be only temporary. Once you have mastered your budget and expanded your financial margin, you will have greater freedom and more choices.

YOUR BUDGETING ACTION STEPS

• The days of scratching out a budget on the back of an envelope are over. Through the internet you have access to a number of free tools or programs that will enable you to formalize the budget process and track your progress in real time. Download an electronic budgeting spreadsheet (Excel), or a personal finance software program such as Mint.com.

• Establish a monthly surplus goal for giving and for saving with the idea that goals are set to be met.

• Make a complete list of your needs (essential expenses) and wants (non-essential expenses). After totaling your essential expenses, add your surplus goal. That becomes your base target. Then add non-essential expenses until you reach your income limit. If your essential expenses exceed your income limit, it would be important to find a way to add income (part-time job, work overtime), or become more frugal with your essential expenses.

• Track your spending. At first, you should track your spending on a daily basis. Or, at the very least, on a weekly basis. Once you master your budgeting, monthly monitoring will be sufficient to ensure you stay on track.

• Look ahead. Using an electronic budgeting spreadsheet or an online personal finance program, you will be able to see how your cash flow picture changes in the months ahead. The goal, of course, is to see how much you can grow your surplus.

DEBT

The rich rules over the poor, and the borrower becomes the lender's slave. [Proverbs 22:7]

In the unrelenting pursuit of more, indulgent spending almost always begets debt, and debt begets financial bondage. This is the situation in which more than 50 percent of Americans find themselves.[4] Astonishingly, the average credit card debt of American households is over $15,000.[5] For many of them, it will take more than thirty years to pay off that high-interest debt.[4] This is remarkable, considering that just a couple of decades ago, credit cards were a tool for only the affluent.

Today almost anyone can get a credit card, and nearly anything can be purchased with little or no down payment. "Buy Now–Pay Later" signs abound, luring millions of cash-strapped people into debt traps. Even the affluent have been caught in the debt spiral

---

4 Federal Reserve G-19 Consumer Credit Report. January 2013. (As of January 2013, Americans held $850.9 billion in credit card debt or $6,920 per household; $1.944 trillion in school, auto, furniture loans, or $15,800 per household.)

5 American Consumer Credit Counseling (ACCC). ConsumerCredit.com, Debt Payoff Calculator ($15,000 of debt at an assumed rate of 12 percent and a minimum monthly payment of $15).

that sprang up with zero-down mortgages for "McMansions" they couldn't afford and that are now upside down.

GOOD DEBT VS. BAD DEBT

Debt used unwisely rarely leads to anything good. This doesn't mean that all debt is necessarily bad and that we shouldn't borrow. Although the Bible teaches that we should be free of debt, it can be used for good sometimes. Knowing the difference between "good" debt and "bad" debt, is a big step toward avoiding the debt spiral that engulfs so many people.

- Good debt can make money: A growing business often needs capital in order to expand, and the only available source might be a loan. For business owners who truly understand their business and their market, the best investment they can make is in their own business.

- Good debt buys appreciating assets: This is, of course, generally true when you buy a house; although recent experience has shown that a prudent approach is required to prevent a good debt from turning into a bad debt. Buying more house than you can afford, or putting little or no money down is not a responsible use of debt. This is also true if you use leverage to purchase stocks. Debt increases the risks and costs associated with equities, and there are no guarantees your investment will outperform your interest costs.

- Good debt pays for good things: Although the Bible advises us not to take on any debt, we are sometimes compelled to follow an opportunity, even though we may not have the capital available. Debt used to further the opportunities for prosperity, such as a college education or an investment in a career, can be good if it is reasonable for your financial situation.

- Bad debt pays for consumable products: When debt is used to buy everyday items such as groceries, clothing, household goods or even cars, there is little or nothing of value after they are consumed; yet, the debt often remains.

- Bad debt pays for things you can't afford: One of the reasons people use credit cards or take out loans is to buy things they can't otherwise afford with money from their existing cash flow or savings. And, as it happens, most of the things bought on credit are "nice- to-have" not "need-to-have," which makes the debt even worse.

SHOULD I USE CREDIT CARDS?

The prudent sees the evil and hides himself, but the naive go on, and are punished for it. [Proverbs 22:3]

There is nothing inherently wrong with using credit cards if you do it responsibly. Credit cards are not the problem; rather it is their misuse that usually leads to the problem.

Most people would find it difficult to go through life without a credit card. They are essential for travel, in order to hold a hotel room or a rental car. They're very convenient and can get you through a checkout line faster than cash. They offer protections against fraud and loss. They can even be very effective cash management tools if you use them strictly to purchase budgeted items with the intent of paying the balance in full each month.

Do not be among those who give pledges, among those who become guarantors for debts. If you have nothing with which to pay, why should he take your bed from under you? [Proverbs 22:26-27]

It's when you use them to buy things that you can't otherwise afford that they begin to enslave you. Even if you can afford the payments, it doesn't mean you should buy something that you could otherwise pay for in the future from accumulated surplus.

YOUR GOOD NAME IS MORE VALUABLE THAN MONEY

A good name is to be more desired than great wealth, favor is better than silver and gold. [Proverbs 22:1]

Building a solid credit history takes years, but it only takes a brief lapse in judgment to ruin it. Your good name and reputation are worth far more to you than a temporary indulgence or life- style urge that could lead to financial stress.

BECOME KNOWLEDGEABLE ABOUT DEBT

The naive believes everything, but the sensible man considers his steps. [Proverbs 14:15]

Even the learned among us can often be naive or ignorant when it comes to borrowing and debt. A loan or a credit card agreement has a lot of moving parts, and many people haven't the foggiest idea of how they work. People who focus on the monthly payment, as opposed to the total cost of the debt, only see the tip of the iceberg – disaster awaits them below the surface.

GETTING OUT OF DEBT

Then she came and told the man of God. And he said, "Go, sell the oil and pay your debt, and you and your sons can live on the rest." [2 Kings 4:7]

From everything we can gather from the Bible, in the eyes of God, debt is not normal. This obviously contradicts the world view that sees it not only as perfectly normal, but essential to making the world go round. But, as with anything in life, just because everyone else is doing it doesn't make it right. We all should do whatever it takes to get out of debt and stay out. That's not just a Christian doctrine, that's a financial survival doctrine.

If you are in over your head in debt, it is important to seek the help of a certified debt counselor. However, if you can still see a light at the end of the tunnel, you should be able to manage your own debt reduction; but it will take determination and discipline.

And do not be conformed to this world, but be transformed by the renewing of your mind, so that you may prove what the will of God is, that which is good and acceptable and perfect. [Romans 12:2]

The first and most important step is to get control of your spending and develop a strict but realistic budget (see Chapter 1). You could go as far as cutting up your credit cards, but the real determinant in whether you succeed is your self-discipline. Set a goal, develop a budget, monitor your spending, and do not deviate.

The Lord will open for you His good storehouse, the heavens, to give rain to your land in its season and to bless all of the work of your hand; and you shall lend to many nations, but you shall not borrow. [Deuteronomy 28:12]

Most people aspire to live debt-free, which, as it happens, is also God's plan for us. He truly wants each of us to thrive and be prosperous and to use our blessings to help others. That can't happen if we are not in the financial position to allow it.

The best way to control debt is to not get into debt to begin with; and if you are in debt, do not add more debt. God's directive for each of us is to wait patiently for His provision based on His timing. Before taking on new debt, He would have us reflect, pray and wait, so He can provide. Those who wait for God's provision will find it in any number of ways, such as an increase income or a better alternative.

It is important to remember, however, that God's provisions are for meeting our essential needs, not our desires. When you use your free will to buy now and pay later, you take on the full responsibility of your actions. But, when you learn to be content with what you have, you can expect that He won't forsake you.

YOUR DEBT CONTROL ACTION STEPS

- Most people in debt don't have a revenue problem, they have a spending problem. Get it under control.

- To pay off debt more quickly, live below your means. Set a goal, establish a budget, and stick to it.

- Use credit cards for budgeted purchases only.

- Carry one, zero-balance credit card only.

- Stop credit card offers by calling 888 5-OPT OUT.

- Don't open a new credit account unless you have a specific use for it and are able to use it responsibly.

SAVING

There is precious treasure and oil in the dwelling of the wise, but a foolish man swallows it up. [Proverbs 21:20]

That the majority of Americans admit they are unprepared for retirement is not at all shocking when you consider the results of another survey conducted by EBRI in which more than half of workers report they have less than $25,000 in savings and investments; and more than a quarter report that they have saved less than $1,000.[6] The numbers improve only slightly for workers closer to retirement. In a 2010 Wells Fargo survey, workers in their fifties who earned below $100,000 had median retirement savings of just $25,000, and those in their sixties had accumulated $30,000. Of all workers surveyed, only 11 percent claim to have saved more than $250,000 for retirement.[7]

Such dismal numbers can be attributed in part to the decimation of retirement accounts caused by the two stock market crashes of the 2000 decade; however, according to a number of studies, that may have accounted for only a small portion of the savings shortfalls. The primary cause can be found in the

6 Employee Benefit Research Institute. 2013 Retirement Confidence Survey.
7 2010 Wells Fargo Retirement Fitness Survey. www.WellsFargo.com

declining savings rate that occurred over three decades, from the 1980s to the end of the 2000 decade. The U.S. Department of Commerce reports that the personal savings rate has been declining steadily, from a high of nearly 12 percent in the mid 1980s to a negative 1.8 percent in 2007.

TRAPPED BY DELUSIONS OF WEALTH AND SECURITY

Much of this decline can be attributed to what some behavioral economists call the "wealth effect," born out of the massive asset appreciation of equities and real estate, and the increased availability of low-cost credit. Essentially, people (Baby Boomers especially) didn't feel the need to save. They believed that their burgeoning 401(k) plans and home equity values would be sufficient to carry them into retirement. So their attention turned to consumption and living the good life in the here and now.

Although the 2008 stock market crash and recession spurred a new awakening for retirement savers of all ages, the current savings rate still sits at a meager 4.6 percent.[8] According to Bankrate's Financial Security Index, nearly 30 percent of Americans have no money saved for emergencies, and of the 70 percent who do, nearly half have only saved enough to cover three month's worth of living expenses. Incredibly, 9 percent of high-income earners have no emergency fund. While many Americans have used their surplus cash flow to pay down debt, which is laudable, too many are still using debt to fund their lifestyle choices.

---

8 U.S. Department of Commerce: Bureau of Economic Analysis. 2013 http://research.stlouisfed.org

SAVING FOR THE FUTURE

Go to the ant, O sluggard, observe her ways and be wise, which, having no chief, officer or ruler, prepares her food in the summer and gathers her provision in the harvest. [Proverbs 6:6-8]

Throughout the Bible the Proverbs cite the need to save for the lean times, often pitting the wise against the foolish in making their case. One of earliest references is found in the Old Testament when Joseph wisely gathered up all of the grains in Egypt prior to the famine, enabling his people to not only survive the emergency, but to flourish after it passed.

Of course, most of us don't need the Bible to tell us that it's wise to save for the future. We know this is true. However, the statistics seem to tell us that there is a huge disconnect between what we all know is true and what we actually do.

When asked why they don't save, people will offer a number of reasons, with "not enough money" being the most prevalent. But even those who live just above the poverty line could manage to save $5 a month. What it comes down to for most people is that they think they have time. "What's one more day (or month, or year)?"

ALL WE REALLY HAVE IS TIME

He who watches the wind will not sow and he who looks at the clouds will not reap. [Ecclesiastes 11:4]

What these people fail to grasp is that time is wasting. The more time you have, the less costly your financial goals are.

For example, if a 25 year-old man wants to save $500,000 for retirement at age 65, and he could earn 6 percent on his money, his monthly savings amount would be $260, if he starts saving now. However, if he waits until age 35 to start saving his monthly savings requirement would nearly double to $510 per month. If he waits until age 45 to begin saving, the amount will double again to $1,100.

THE ADVANTAGE OF SAVING EARLY AND SAVING OFTEN

The opportunity of saving early is best illustrated with numbers. Take, for example, Linda and George. Linda invests $20,000 per year from ages 25 to 45, and then she stops contributing to her savings. George doesn't invest from ages 25 to 45, but he then invests $20,000 per year from ages 45 to 65. Assuming an investment return of 6 percent, by age 65, Linda would have $2,500,000, whereas George would only have $790,000!

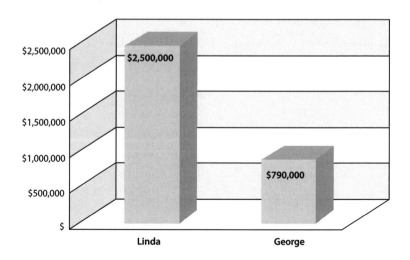

Steady plodding brings prosperity; hasty speculation brings poverty. [Proverbs 21:5]

The point is clear. Time has value, and the cost of waiting can be prohibitively expensive. The longer you wait the more it will cost you to reach your goal. Or, you will need to take greater risks, which few people want to do with their financial future.

SAVING FOR A PURPOSE

One of the biggest challenges for savers is staying motivated, which is what feeds the discipline needed for saving. Saving money just for the sake of savings doesn't always provide the inspiration people need to keep saving. Also, the Bible makes the distinction between saving and hoarding – encouraging the former and frowning upon the latter. Money that is hoarded rather than saved is usually not allocated to any particular need, now or in the future, and God looks at that as hoarding in order to enrich our lives with no higher purpose.

But God said to him, 'You fool! This very night your soul is required of you; and now who will own what you have prepared?' So is the man who stores up treasure for himself, and is not rich toward God." [Luke 12:20-21]

But, when you set a goal, and achieving it is of paramount importance to you, it suddenly becomes easier to save.

Another challenge arises if you have multiple goals you must achieve. Retirement is an important goal for most people, but, typically, there are multiple, shorter term goals that are more pressing. Such as establishing an emergency fund to buy a home or a car, or funding a college education. Combining your savings into one account is like lumping all of your goals together, which makes it difficult to track them.

With the availability of online savings accounts; it is possible to establish multiple accounts, each dedicated to a separate goal that can be tracked and managed individually toward that goal. This will ensure that you don't lose sight of your priorities, and as your financial circumstances change, you can manage your allocations among the accounts to reflect your current needs.

SAVE FOR SPECIFIC GOALS

Most savings institutions offer a range of savings vehicles from which to choose. Each vehicle has a different set of savings characteristics that vary depending on the time horizon of the deposit. Some vehicles are more suited for short-term needs, while others are ideal for long-term savings needs.

Emergency Fund: It is universally recommended that you have an emergency fund consisting of short-term savings that could cover at least six months of living expenses in the event of a loss of income. There really is no better alternative than a savings account. The minimum initial deposit is low, and with most accounts, there is no minimum balance required. In most types of savings accounts, Federal Reserve Board Regulation D, limits the number of withdrawals from your account six times or more a year.

Saving for a Home: If your savings goal is farther out, say, three to five years, you may want your money to earn money market rates while you still have short-term access. Money market accounts typically require a higher minimum deposit ($2,500) and a minimum balance, so they are more suited for larger savings needs. Some money market accounts even have check writing privileges; however, withdrawals are limited.

Saving for Retirement: If your time horizon is beyond five years, you can potentially maximize your return by investing in five to 10-year certificates of deposits (CDs). CDs are issued with varying maturity dates; the longer term maturities generally have higher rates of interest although some banks do run promotions offering higher rates on shorter term maturities. As long as you have a liquid savings account for short-term needs, you could consider investing in the longer maturities.

SAVING FROM THE HEART

So then, while we have opportunity, let us do good to all people, and especially to those who are of the household of the faith. [Galatians 6:10]

We are asked to first provide our tithe and then pay ourselves with savings, even before we pay our bills. After we pay our creditors, our next obligation is to use our surplus to meet the needs of others. Jesus asks us where our heart lies:

"Do not store up for yourselves treasures on earth, where moth and rust destroy, and where thieves break in and steal. But store up for yourselves treasures in heaven, where neither moth nor rust destroys, and where thieves do not break in or steal; for where your treasure is, there your heart will be also." [Matthew 6:19-21]

Done right, your savings and your ability to save will both increase over time. And there will come a time when your surplus will exceed your needs. The Bible tells us that, if we choose to not put a cap on our savings, then we are, by default, choosing to keep our treasures temporarily here on earth. But, if we deliberately set a maximum savings goal, and help others in need, we are intentionally leaving our treasure in heaven. That's why it's important to constantly remind ourselves whether we're saving for a purpose or if we're hoarding simply for the love of money.

YOUR SAVINGS ACTION STEPS:

- **Set your goals**: What are you saving for? An emergency fund? Retirement? A new car? Set your goal, which should include a time horizon.

- **Establish a strict budget**: You can't save if you don't budget. After your tithe, pay yourself first.

- **Begin with a tithe**: By tithing first, you will ensure that you're building your treasure in heaven.

- **Live within your means**: Make the distinction between what you actually need and what is strictly a desire. Do you really need the latest model car with leather seats? Do you really need granite counters in your kitchen? Your lifestyle choices will determine your ability to save.

- **Protect what you have**: The purpose of insurance is to transfer risks that you can't pay for to someone who can until you can accumulate your own capital. Make sure you have full coverage for your car, your house, your income (including disability insurance), your assets (liability and long-term care insurance), and your family (life insurance).

Chapter Four

GIVING

In everything I showed you that by working hard in this manner you must help the weak and remember the words of the Lord Jesus, that He Himself said, 'It is more blessed to give than to receive.' [Acts 20:35]

When disaster or tragedy strikes, that puts people in danger. There is no other nation on earth where you'd want to be than the United States. We are indeed very fortunate to live in the most generous country on the planet. But, while we should celebrate the collective generosity of our nation, we should also examine our individual propensity to give and whether it stands up to the test of God's principles. Although 25 percent of Americans view themselves as regular churchgoers, 45 percent of adults have reduced or stopped tithing regularly to their church in 2012. According to a study conducted by the Barma Group[9], that's up from 37 percent in 2011.

Unquestionably, the economic downturn has influenced the rate of giving. The Barma study shows that more than 30 percent of people who tithe or donate regularly to their church have cut back because of their own financial difficulties and 25

9 Barna Group. April 2012. The Economy Continues to Squeeze American's Charitable Giving. www.barna.org

percent have stopped donating to churches altogether; and 48 percent have reduced or stopped their charitable donations to other non-profit groups.

While it is difficult to find fault with a struggling family trying to make ends meet, the Barma study revealed more about the underlying attitudes and generosity of Americans. At the end of the day, "Most Americans think of their giving as secondary to their survival. Yet, from a Biblical perspective, generosity should be part of Christian's fundamental response to the downturn."

Is it wrong that we first consider our own plight in determining whether we are able to give? The Bible tells us that it is not always the size or form of the gift, but the sacrifice that speaks the loudest. Consider this story of the poor widow:

> *And He sat down opposite the treasury, and began observing how the people were putting money into the treasury; and many rich people were putting in large sums. A poor widow came and put in two small copper coins, which amount to a cent. Calling His disciples to Him, He said to them, "Truly I say to you, this poor widow put in more than all the contributors to the treasury; for they all put in out of their surplus, but she, out of her poverty, put in all she owned, all she had to live on."* [Mark 12:41-45]

You don't have to be wealthy to share yourself with others. And, certainly, those with less to give are making a much greater sacrifice than those who have more to give. Heartfelt giving of one's time and energy in acts of kindness and service to others will earn God's rewards as surely as giving money.

*Each one must do just as he has purposed in his heart, not
grudgingly or under compulsion, for God loves a cheerful giver.*
[2 Corinthians 9:7]

HOW MUCH IS ENOUGH?

The figures are mixed on how much the wealthy give to charities. In the 2012 Bank of America Study of High Net Worth
Philanthropy, it was found that millionaires give about 9
percent of their income to charities. But another study, conducted by the Chronicle of Philanthropy, showed that people
who make more than $100,000 give less than 4.2 percent.
That might make one conclude that the more money a household earns the more it will give; except for the fact that the
same study revealed that households earning between $50,000
and $75,000 give an average of 7.6 percent to charity. So how
much is enough when it comes to giving?

John D. Rockefeller gave 10 percent of his income to charity from the very first dollar he earned until his last. Warren
Buffet challenges all billionaires to give half of their wealth to
charity. So, how should the rest of us mere mortals demonstrate our generosity? How do we put a percentage on what it
means to be generous?

Your search for the answers should begin with the Bible, which
has plenty to say about giving and generosity.

THE PRINCIPLE OF TITHING

*"Bring the whole tithe into the storehouse, so that there may
be food in My house, and test Me now in this," says the* LORD

of hosts, "if I will not open for you the windows of heaven and pour out for you a blessing until it overflows." [Malachi 3:10]

The Old Testament establishes the principle of "tithing" – giving one-tenth of your income to the church – with God's promise that you will be blessed. Many Christians today argue that the tithing law of the Old Testament, which commanded the Jews to give one-tenth of their goods to God, does not apply in the faith based teaching of the New Testament. So compulsory tithing has become a subject of spirited debates among Christians throughout the country.

While it's true that the New Testament doesn't command a tithe, some argue that He at least endorsed it:

"Woe to you, scribes and Pharisees, hypocrites! For you tithe mint and dill and cummin, and have neglected the weightier provisions of the law: justice and mercy and faithfulness; but these are the things you should have done without neglecting the others." [Matthew 23:23]

THE NEW COVENANT OF GIVING

But others point out that, as a Jew, Jesus was bound by the laws of the Old Testament. And when He gave His life, a new covenant with God was established, as written in the New Testament. The new covenant makes no mention of a tithing law; rather it teaches us to *"put aside and save, as he may prosper"* (1 Corinthians 16:2), and that *"Each one must do just as he has purposed in his heart, not grudgingly or under compulsion, for God loves a cheerful giver"* (2 Corinthians 9:7). This, the New Testament teaches us, will *"prove through the earnestness of others the sincerity of your love also"* (2 Corinthians 8:8).

The New Testament espouses giving one's heart in whatever form generosity might take. To do otherwise, by compulsion or grudgingly would be a sin.

> *Now this I say, he who sows sparingly will also reap sparingly, and he who sows bountifully will also reap bountifully. Each one must do just as he has purposed in his heart, not grudgingly or under compulsion, for God loves a cheerful giver.* [2 Corinthians 9:6-7]

The overriding principle of the New Testament, and the one which guides our conscience in giving, is that God owns everything and we are merely His stewards here on earth. To give 10 percent, or 90 percent back to the Lord, is simply a return of what already belongs to Him. This is not a command of God; rather it is an attitude He instills that enables us to give generously, cheerfully, and according to our prosperity.

> *The generous man will be prosperous, and he who waters will himself be watered.* [Proverbs 11:25]

So, in essence, the tithing debate becomes moot. Whether you ascribe to the one-tenth tenet or not, the new covenant actually raises the bar on giving and issues us a higher calling with increased responsibilities. We don't need to get caught up in percentages or obsessing over what is required of us. Instead, we are called to take our minds off of our earthly possessions and subordinate our ambitions and motives to God's plan for us. For what He did in offering His greatest possession, His Son, to save us, He asks us to sow into things that will have eternal value.

So, how much is enough?

Therefore if you have not been faithful in the use of unrighteous wealth, who will entrust the true riches to you? [Luke 16:11]

Going back to the story of the poor widow who sacrificed her coins for the temple treasury, the answer lies not in an amount or a percentage, but rather, in your mindset and your faith. God looks upon your mercy as having more value than money. As to gifts of charity, God simply asks that we give according to our ability, and for that we will be blessed accordingly. His "law" states simply:

Give, and it will be given to you. They will pour into your lap a good measure—pressed down, shaken together, and running over. For by your standard of measure it will be measured to you in return." [Luke 6:38]

God challenges us to "test" Him in His promise to bring blessings upon those who give willingly. You might even look at it as a series of tests that take you along a progression. Pass the first test by giving what you can no matter how small the amount and you move on to the next level. The example of John D. Rockefeller earlier in this chapter best illustrates how the progression of giving can translate into bigger blessings.

"I never would have been able to tithe the first million dollars I ever made if I had not tithed my first salary, which was $1.50 per week." – John D. Rockefeller

All of this is not to say that we should abandon the principle of tithing. Whatever your stand on it, it does provide a standard by which you can manage your budget. It makes it easier to make the lifestyle choices that will ensure you can remain faithful to God. And, by no means should it limit you if your prosperity enables you to increase your giving.

WE HAVE RESPONSIBILITIES

> *From everyone who has been given much, much will be required; and to whom they entrusted much, of him they will ask all the more.* [*Luke 12:48*]

Whether you tithe or give freely according to your ability, it is only the beginning of your stewardship. We are partners with God in the management of His resources. Just because we put something in the plate on Sunday doesn't mean we can leave it all to God to do the rest.

> *Even so faith, if it has no works, is dead, being by itself.* [James 2:17]

Giving is an act of faith, but God expects us to walk the talk by taking action when the opportunities He provides present themselves. It might be a better job opportunity or the chance to improve your skills. Maybe it will be in the form of a revelation about your finances to help you save more money. And, of course, God also expects us to be effective managers of the 90 percent, or whatever amount of His resources you choose to keep for yourself. The "test" is your ability to take action at the appropriate times while successfully managing what He has entrusted to you. Pass the tests and God says He will entrust you with more.

His master said to him, 'Well done, good and faithful slave. You were faithful with a few things, I will put you in charge of many things; enter into the joy of your master.'
[Matthew 25:23]

Budget, plan, and work like your financial success is all up to you. If you do your part, God will do His.

ACTION STEPS FOR PLANNED GIVING

• Examine your motivations for giving. If they're not from your heart, pray for God's guidance.

• Incorporate your giving as a definite part of your budget.

• Give "off the top" (like our bills) at the beginning of the month, pay-period, etc.

• Find several ways to give each month - money, clothes, food, and time.

• Serve and support your local church and other charitable organizations.

• Whatever portion of your income you are able to give right now, make a commitment to increase that portion as you increase your income.

Chapter Five

CONTENTMENT

The Lord is my shepherd, I shall not want. [Psalm 23:1]

In designing your ambition for a good life, it comes down to having clarity in your beliefs and values. But more important, it needs to be placed in a context that clearly addresses the question: "But for the sake of what?" What do you believe, value and care for? These are the primary elements at the heart of a good life. These differentiate it from a philosophy of "more." Money can certainly help create certain positive situations in our life, but it can never bring the fulfillment people seek.

Take a moment and think back to a time when you were earning 30 percent less income. Were you happy then? Most people would tend to say "yes." For those who answer "no," the chances are that, if they weren't happy then, they aren't happy now. For the rest of us, more money and spending didn't necessarily improve our happiness.

Now think about the next 30 percent increase in income you might receive. When people receive a pay raise, the rational and responsible action to take would be to increase their giving and savings by that amount, or at least proportionately.

However, for most people, especially those without a clear vision or plan for the future, the typical response is to add the pay raise to their lifestyle at the expense of savings.

Typically, people who don't have a "purpose" for the next dollars they earn will likely give into the cultural tendency toward "more is better," with the expectation that it will make them happier to make relative improvements in their lifestyle. The reality is that the happiness of consumption is fleeting and does little to improve a person's sense of overall well-being.

LEARNING CONTENTMENT

For we have brought nothing into the world, so we cannot take anything out of it either. If we have food and covering, with these we shall be content. But those who want to get rich fall into temptation and a snare and many foolish and harmful desires which plunge men into ruin and destruction. [1 Timothy 6:7-9]

Of all the financial directives found in the Bible, *contentment* probably produces the greatest amount of angst in people, because it forces us to question our lifestyle decisions. But the contentment conversation is not about whether we are satisfied in life; rather it centers on whether we understand God's plan for our life and have the conviction to follow it.

We live our lives at digital speed, and the demands of work and family can easily consume our time and thoughts. So it's not uncommon for people to suddenly find themselves aimlessly pursuing more without regard for its purpose. Then there is the tendency for people to almost mindlessly adjust their lifestyle to keep up with the Jones. We might try to avoid both of these digressions, but unless we are constantly focused on God's plans for us, and have faith in His ability to provide, it becomes too easy to slide into discontentment.

For some affluent people, discontentment comes not from lacking material possessions; rather it comes from the anxiety about the possibility of losing their possessions. People who have an unhealthy attachment to their possessions and money will never find contentment for fear that they could one day be taken from them. Contentment will always elude them because they can't find it by adding more possessions, and they will suffer extreme discontentment should they lose any of what they have. Conversely, people who understand God's plans for them are willing to lose what they have because they know they can find contentment in what He provides.

But godliness actually is a means of great gain when accompanied by contentment. [1 Timothy 6:6]

We can all agree that managing money when you have little of it is different than when you have a lot of it. But there is little to differentiate between the contentment that Bill Gates seeks and that which you and I seek. Some of us are fortunate to have experienced life on both ends of the spectrum. Perhaps not at the level of Bill Gates, or a homeless person, but certainly at a lifestyle range that reflects the *haves* and the *have nots*. In the roaring 1980s and 1990s it was the young upwardly mobile professionals (Yuppies) who strived to live life in prosperity based in large part on what was to come – higher earnings, stock options, high investment returns, etc.

For many people of that period, the race to upgrade their lifestyle defined their lives. Conversations centered on what people bought over the weekend and often turned toward something else they would like to buy. This is evidence that happiness derived from buying things is fleeting at best.

Then He said to them, "Beware, and be on your guard against every form of greed; for not even when one has an abundance does his life consist of his possessions." [Luke 12:15]

Then came the 2000 decade, with its busts and crashes that brought many young professionals, now more appropriately aligned with the Baby Boom generation, back to earth. Yet, having lived the high life, many of those who lost their assets or their jobs were unable to adjust to a more humble lifestyle, choosing instead to live a life of financial deception. Many people turned to borrowing and highly leveraged real estate in order to maintain the fantasy of prosperity. And we all know what transpired near the end of the decade – a record number of bankruptcies, foreclosures and people unemployed.

LESSONS LEARNED?

The recent economic downturn appears to have had a profound effect on the lives of millions of Americans. Many have adopted new financial principles as they adjust for what many are calling the "new normal" economy. Suddenly, living within one's means has become a more socially acceptable, and living with debt is no longer considered a fact of life. "Downsizing," as in going small with housing and cars, is the new catchword. Even the affluent are embracing the new trend toward frugality. But how many are doing so purely out of financial necessity, and how many have learned contentment as espoused in the Bible?

More than three years into a sluggish economic recovery and despite lifestyle and financial management adjustments, the confidence of most Americans continues to slide into uncharted depths. The 2012 Retirement Confidence Survey, co-sponsored by the EBRI, reveals that only 14 percent of today's workers are very confident that they will have enough money to live comfortably throughout their retirement years. That's down substantially from confidence level highs of 27 percent prior to the 2008 stock market crash, and is the lowest in the survey's 22 year history.

Current retirees are only slightly more confident, with 21 percent seeing clear to their life-time income needs. But what isn't clear is whether that confidence is based on their certainty of outcome, or the strength of their faith that things will work out as hoped.

CONFIDENCE AND CONTENTMENT GO HAND-IN-HAND

If you make lifestyle changes purely out of financial necessity, chances are you are still focus on what you have and don't have. You may accept your new standing, but true happiness will be elusive if you continue to look toward external things to bring you satisfaction. And, if you place your ultimate trust in the economy, the markets, and your bank account, your confidence of getting what you need in the future will diminish. Simply put, if you can't be happy in your current lifestyle, you can be fairly certain you won't happy in the future, and that's a tragedy.

If instead, you allow your lifestyle changes to be guided by the financial principles of the Bible, and learn how to find contentment in knowing that God has given us what He knows we need, then happiness becomes a natural by-product. And, if you are content with knowing that God has a plan for you, your confidence in the future will be brimming.

Not that I speak from want, for I have learned to be content in whatever circumstances I am. I know how to get along with humble means, and I also know how to live in prosperity; in any and every circumstance I have learned the secret of being filled and going hungry, both of having abundance and suffering need. I can do all things through Him who strengthens me. [Philippians 4:11-13]

We all have the opportunity to learn the lessons of the past and from those who couldn't find contentment in their present circumstances. Seeking contentment shouldn't be confused with accepting mediocrity. God wants us to work hard and diligently toward prosperity. And to be content does not mean to be satisfied with what you have. Contentment is a feeling in your heart that you are thankful for what God has provided. It is your faith in the future that everything will be all right.

Make sure that your character is free from the love of money, being content with what you have; for He Himself has said, "I will never desert you, nor will I ever forsake you." [Hebrews 13:5]

YOUR ACTION STEPS FOR LEARNING CONTENTMENT

1. Review the financial principles of the Bible in the Introduction.

    - Establish a strict budget and learn to live within your means.

    - Live debt-free.

    - Focus on building your reserves.

    - Establish meaningful long-term goals.

    - Seek good financial counsel.

2. Establish a habit of giving.

3. Prioritize your life and determine what really matters. Make every day a Thanksgiving to God.

4. Know God's plan and have faith in the future. We don't know exactly how things will turn out; we just know that they will turn out all right.

And the peace of God, which surpasses all comprehension, will guard your hearts and your minds in Christ Jesus. [Philippians 4:7]

Chapter Six

PLANNING

It wasn't long ago that financial planning was thought of as a discipline that only applied to the very wealthy. Most people didn't feel the need to plan, and, frankly, most financial advisors felt the same way. If you consider the fact that, just a few decades ago, the average life expectancy was just 74 years, few people were concerned with making their retirement income last a lifetime. Back then, the majority of retirees were supported by the three-legged stool of Social Security, personal savings, <u>and</u> guaranteed pensions.

But much has changed in just the last fifteen years. The need for financial planning has been extended to everyone who hopes to achieve their most important goals and secure their financial future. Consider how our financial world has evolved:

- Life expectancy took a huge leap in the last twenty years, with average life spans increasing to 85 years and an increasing number of people living into their 90s.[10] Add that to the continued extinction of guaranteed pension plans, and suddenly people are concerned about outliving their resources.

---

10 Social Security Administration. Life Expectancy for Retirement and Survivor Benefits. www.socialsecurity.gov

- Health care costs have more than doubled over the last few decades, threatening to consume as much as one-third of a retiree's resources.[11]

- The near vertical trajectory of the stock market of the 1980s and 1990s has become, to many people, a sadistic roller coaster ride they would rather not have to stomach.

- The proliferation of investment products and providers over the last couple of decades has created too many choices, which have led to confusion, and, ultimately, investment paralysis.

- College tuition continues to climb out of the reach of many American families.

- Over the last twenty years, our tax code has become, arguably, one of the most complex in the world.

Of course, these developments, as well as the ongoing evolution of the financial world, affect all of us; but the paradox of wealth accumulation is that the better you do, the more complicated your needs become. And there is an additional layer of complexity in providing for longer life spans: higher health costs, lower earnings, smaller pensions, and fewer accumulated assets.

WHAT THE BIBLE SAYS ABOUT PLANNING

But with complexity comes confusion, and confusion leads to fear, and fear leads to inaction. So many people, paralyzed by fear, are more content to worry about their future than to plan for it. But doesn't the Bible teach us not to worry about the future, not to worry about our needs being met, not to be fear-

11 2013 Milliman Medical Index. www.Milliman.com

ful? Wouldn't planning and saving for the future, therefore, be an act of distrust in God?

> *But seek first His kingdom and His righteousness, and all these things will be added to you. "So do not worry about tomorrow; for tomorrow will care for itself. Each day has enough trouble of its own.* [Matthew 6:33-34]

While we can conclude that we are called to trust in God to provide all that we need, that is the precise reason why we also need to be the best stewards of what He has entrusted to us. Too often, people use scripture as an excuse or a rationale for not planning or saving; or they allow their fears to control their decisions, which are then made in haste or without regard for the fundamental principles espoused in the Bible.

Indeed, the Bible is laden with examples of God's admonishments for the lazy or inattentive who fail to prepare for the future....

> *Go to the ant, O sluggard, observe her ways and be wise, which, having no chief, officer or ruler, prepares her food in the summer and gathers her provision in the harvest.* [Proverbs 6:6-8]

....and encouragement for the diligent:

The plans of the diligent lead surely to advantage, but everyone who is hasty comes surely to poverty. [Proverbs 21:5]

GOD WANTS US TO PLAN AND PREPARE

The mind of man plans his way, but the LORD directs his steps. [Proverbs 16:9]

Clearly, God wants us to plan and to be prepared, but to do so with His guidance and our adherence to the Biblical principles for financial management (as outlined in Chapter 1):

Principle #1: Live Within Your Means

Principle #2: Live Debt-Free

Principle #3: Build Reserves

Principle #4: Establish Long-term Goals

Principle #5: Seek Financial Counsel

These principles, which are supported with a multitude of scriptures throughout the Bible, serve as a framework for doing God's will in pursuit of one's personal financial freedom. The underlying premise of these enduring principles is that, if you are slave to debt or the need for money, you will be less able to focus your energies and your resources on doing God's work.

In essence, the Bible is a financial planning guide that asks us to believe in these principles so that we can be effective stewards of His property. And, not unlike the financial advisors of today, the Bible offers very specific advice on how to plan for the future. Consider these sage pieces of advice:

SET PRIORITIES

Prepare your work outside and make it ready for yourself in the field; afterwards, then, build your house. [Proverbs 24:27]

Financial advisors will tell you that you must set priorities and address them in order. If a priority is essential, don't be distracted by things that aren't as important. While building a barn is important, a farmer who tends to that first would miss the chance to plant for the season. In the end, he would have a barn, but no crops to store. When we try to do everything at once instead of focusing on priorities, we tend to spread ourselves too thin, and then nothing gets done, or it gets done poorly.

REDUCE YOUR RISK

The prudent sees the evil and hides himself, but the naive go on, and are punished for it. [Proverbs 22:3]

Risks are all around us: market risk, inflation risk, interest rate risk, and longevity risk. No matter how conservative you might be in your investment philosophy, if you don't take measures to reduce your risk in these areas, your savings are vulnerable. Those who ignore or inadequately prepare for these risks will suffer consequences.

COUNT ON CHANGE

Come now, you who say, "Today or tomorrow we will go to such and such a city, and spend a year there and engage in business and make a profit." Yet you do not know what your life will be like tomorrow. You are just a vapor that appears for a little while and then vanishes away. [James 4:13-14]

We can't possibly know what the future will bring, whether in terms of our own lives, or in the elements around us. What is certain is that we are living on borrowed time and we must make the most of it by making the right decisions.

KNOW HOW MUCH YOUR GOALS WILL COST

For which one of you, when he wants to build a tower, does not first sit down and calculate the cost to see if he has enough to complete it? [Luke 14:28]

One of the first steps in the financial planning process is to calculate the cost of your goals. That entails assessing your present situation and then determining how much you will need to save in order to achieve them.

TAKE ACTION

> *In all labor there is profit, but mere talk leads only to poverty.*
> [Proverbs 14:23]

Plans generally fail because people fail to implement them. The key to successfully implementing a long-term plan is to first set realistic goals and prioritize, and then address one need at a time (depending on your resources). Patience and discipline are essential virtues in order to stick with a plan while holding yourself accountable for its implementation.

A WORD ABOUT INSURANCE

> *But if anyone does not provide for his own, and especially for those of his household, he has denied the faith and is worse than an unbeliever.* [1 Timothy 5:8]

Few people could bear the costs of unexpected events; such as a disability, the death of a family member, a house fire, or a car accident. Such that they wouldn't cause severe or even irreparable harm to their financial well-being. Preparing first for the unexpected allows us to move forward with a greater sense of confidence toward building sufficiency to prepare for what we do expect.

In essence, insurance, in all of its forms, is a plan for the un-expected. For many in the Christian community, this shows a lack of trust in God. But others would contend that it demonstrates proper planning as a faithful steward of His property. Does it show a lack of trust in God to wear a life-vest while river rafting? Are you less faithful when you pack an emergency kit in case of a natural disaster?

In the old days, farmers banded together as a community of "barn raisers," who acted as one to rebuild a barn when one of its member's barns burned to the ground. Building a barn required more skills and materials than any single farmer could provide for himself. So the community provided the capacity to which every farmer contributed and in which they all participated.

An insurance contract is essentially a community transfer of risk in which everyone agrees to contribute to a risk pool so they can participate in a particular outcome. The larger the potential loss is, such as a home, the larger the community that is needed to make the individual contributions affordable. The community has a shared agreement for the outcome, which, in this case, will be to replace the home.

A community for the sake of protection is not limited to insurance. It can be any group of people who come together in order to produce a more effective outcome than they could produce alone. It is through the community that we increase our capacity to handle some of life's complex issues. We continuously draw capacity from the community in our family, our faith, among friends, and in our society; yet we tend not to notice it, except in the worst circumstances. We take for granted many of the protections and efficiencies offered through our communities which often results in their underutilization.

YOUR PLANNING ACTION STEPS:

- Discover your ambition for a "good life" today and in the future.

- Set realistic goals that can be quantified.

- Prioritize your needs and goals and plan to address them in order of importance.

- Assess where you are today financially in relation to where you want to be.

- Assess your ability to tolerate risk, understanding that risk comes in many forms: market risk, inflation risk, taxation risk, interest rate risk, etc.

- Establish a savings and investment program using a diversified and disciplined approach.

- Monitor and measure your progress toward your goals.

- Seek financial counsel with a qualified, independent financial advisor who places your interests first.

Chapter Seven
INVESTING

The plans of the diligent lead surely to advantage, but everyone who is hasty comes surely to poverty. [Proverbs 21:5]

The world of investing has changed dramatically over the last few decades. With the advent of high technology and the incessant quest for profits, the financial services industry has exploded with an ever expanding universe of new investment products and an endless pipeline of information and advice. On the other hand, we have also witnessed the implosion of the financial services industry through a dot com bust, two stock market crashes, and a financial meltdown. One could make the argument that this remarkable chain of financial calamities was driven by a freight train of emotions, fueled by unbridled greed, and finally derailed by sheer panic and fear.

Shell-shocked investors and humbled financial advisors are now returning to the basics of investing that are grounded in age-old investment principles, many of which just happen to have originated in the Bible. Getting back to the basics essentially means rediscovering your purpose for investing, which in Biblical terms means to gain financial security by increasing assets in order to serve God more fully.

Consider the story Jesus relates in the Parable of the Talents:

So He said, "A nobleman went to a distant country to receive a kingdom for himself, and then return. And he called ten of his slaves, and gave them ten minas and said to them, 'Do business with this until I come back.' But his citizens hated him and sent a delegation after him, saying, 'We do not want this man to reign over us.' When he returned, after receiving the kingdom, he ordered that these slaves, to whom he had given the money, be called to him so that he might know what business they had done. The first appeared, saying, Master, your mina has made ten minas more.' And he said to him, 'Well done, good slave, because you have been faithful in a very little thing, you are to be in authority over ten cities.' The second came, saying, 'Your mina, master, has made five minas.' And he said to him also, 'And you are to be over five cities.' Another came, saying, 'Master, here is your mina, which I kept put away in a handkerchief; for I was afraid of you, because you are an exacting man; you take up what you did not lay down and reap what you did not sow.' He said to him, 'By your own words I will judge you, you worthless slave. Did you know that I am an exacting man, taking up what I did not lay down and reaping what I did not sow? Then why did you not put my money in the bank, and having come, I would have collected it with interest?' Then he said to the bystanders, 'Take the mina away from him and give it to the one who has the ten minas.' And they said to him, 'Master, he has ten minas already.' I tell you that to everyone who has, more shall be given, but from the one who does not have, even what he does have shall be taken away." [Luke 19:12-26]

It is God who provides the seed for planting, and if we plant it, He will multiply it. So investing is really based on multiplying assets that God provides, and then turning the crop over to Him while retaining the seed for even greater harvests in the future. The more we demonstrate our faithfulness, the more He will provide.

People who have no real purpose for investing are apt to turn money into objects of devotion and idolatry, substituting the love of money for leading a purposeful life. Although God has nothing against prosperity, He abhors the sins that sometimes accompany it. It's the attitudes of greed, covetousness, and pride that often lead to the downfall of investors whose only purpose is to hoard wealth or to try to get rich quick.

All the ways of a man are clean in his own sight, but the LORD weighs the motives. [Proverbs 16:2]

Investing surpluses for the purpose of providing comfort and convenience for our families, or providing for the needs of others is what God has in mind for us. This then begs the question, "How much is enough?" If you continue to invest and accumulate money beyond that, you must ask yourself the reason. Is it for the love of money, or is it because you fear for the future? God chastises both reasons – the first being a sin, and the second a demonstration of a lack of faith in Him.

But seek first His kingdom and His righteousness, and all these things will be added to you. [Matthew 6:33]

INVEST CONDITIONALLY

Prepare your work outside and make it ready for yourself in the field; afterwards, then, build your house. [Proverbs 24:27]

It's also important to know what you are investing, meaning you shouldn't mix investing with saving. Savings, as described in Chapter 3, are for the explicit purpose of creating the security for meeting emergency needs and other short-term savings goals, such as buying a car. For that, it is always recommended that your savings be placed in safe, liquid instruments, such as savings or money market accounts. For savings goals three to five years out, a CD with a multi-year guarantee can be a better option. Investing in market-based assets, which entails varying degrees of risk, is generally more suitable for longer time horizons to allow time for multiple market cycles.

People who have yet to satisfy the requirements for fully funding a six to twelve-month emergency fund, or paid off high-interest debt, or who haven't yet purchased their protections (life and disability insurance), should attend to these priorities before setting up an investment plan. Investments are considered surplus, over and above what it will take to sustain you and your family now and well into the future. It's what you invest and spend when you know there is no threat to your basic security, and that includes your retirement.

DEVELOP A SOUND INVESTMENT PLAN

In the story of *Alice and Wonderland*, Alice arrives at a fork in the road and wonders aloud which road to take. A smiling Cheshire cat appears and asks her what her destination is. To which she replies, "I don't know." The toothy cat then offers the only possible response, "Well, then it doesn't matter."

While such an exchange may not actually occur in people's lives, there is ample evidence to support that it may occur in people's minds as they consider their future. Numerous surveys show that less than half of adults have yet to clearly define their retirement destination, so it is of little consequence to them which path they take. That can explain, at least in part, the relatively low savings rates among adults today. Without a clear retirement destination, people tend to focus on the here and now, which favors consumption over savings.

Studies clearly show that investors who adhere to a plan with clearly defined objectives and a tailored investment strategy outperform those who don't. A well-conceived investment strategy is what keeps investors from falling into investment traps, such as chasing returns or trying to time the markets.

- Having a plan enables you to stay focused on your individual benchmarks, rather than market benchmarks or indexes, which are meaningless to your long-term strategy.

- A plan keeps you firmly grounded in risk management principles that closely track your personal risk profile while optimizing their asset allocation.

- More important, the plan helps to shield you from the irrational behavior of the herd, which is often driven by euphoria or panic.

APPLYING GOD'S PRINCIPLES

Also it is not good for a person to be without knowledge, and he who hurries his footsteps errs. [Proverbs 19:2]

It can be said that the Bible introduced the very first investment principles, which are as applicable today as they were thousands of years ago. Understanding and applying God's principles in your investment plan can help you avoid the typical mistakes investors make, and that your plan is attuned to the higher purpose of serving God.

Specifically, the Bible cautions us to be wise with our money, and to exercise patience and prudence with the resources that God provides us. The purpose of an investment plan is to instill confidence in your investment decisions and provide the fortitude to stick with your plan. God asks us to take responsibility for making the right decisions on the basis of His principles and assures us that He will provide the returns. In developing and executing our investment plan, we are tasked with five responsibilities:

INVEST ONLY IN WHAT YOU UNDERSTAND

The mind of the prudent acquires knowledge, and the ear of the wise seeks knowledge. [Proverbs 18:15]

Investors throughout the world pine for words of investment wisdom from Warren Buffet, considered to be the most successful investor ever. Next to his very first piece of advice, "Don't lose money," his most quoted counsel is to "invest in what you know." Most people attribute this popular investment principle to Buffet; however, its origin can be found throughout the Bible.

Buffet applies this principle to investing in stocks – understanding how a company makes money and knowing its competitors and the market before owning its stock. But the same principle should be applied to making decisions about the types of investments to own. Investment products and methods have become very complex, which makes it difficult to truly understand how they work. And in the day and age of scams and fraud, what you don't know can hurt you.

Do Not Over-leverage Your Investments

The rich rules over the poor, and the borrower becomes the lender's slave. [Proverbs 22:7]

Some investors have successfully used other people's money to increase their profits on investments. By putting up a small amount of money and borrowing the difference to buy hundreds of shares of stock, or a piece of real estate, an investor can multiply his return if the investment goes up in value. Conversely, should the investment fall in value, the investor could be liable for more than what the investment is worth. Such is the risk of using leverage in investments.

The Bible teaches us that debt is not normal, and that *"the borrower is slave to the lender."* When you borrow money to buy and invest, you don't really own the investment, and your fortunes are subordinate to the lender. When a loss occurs, the investor loses big and the lender is made whole, regardless.

From a purely practical standpoint, incurring debt to make an investment only increases your risk and your costs. If your investment return doesn't outpace your interest costs over time, you will never come out ahead.

Don't Make Hasty Decisions

The plans of the diligent lead surely to advantage, but everyone who is hasty comes surely to poverty. [Proverbs 21:5]

Investment decisions have long-term implications, so you should take time to reflect, pray, and ask for the counsel of others. It is important to consider all options and scrutinize your motives. In investing, exercising patience is less about doing the right thing and more about having the presence of mind to avoid doing the wrong thing. Successful investors are able to withstand the pain of missing some of the upside in the market, or riding out a market decline in order to minimize the typical and often devastating mistakes that unsuccessful investors make.

Patient investors who have faith in God don't know when everything is going to turn out all right; they just know that it will do so eventually. So they invest accordingly.

SEEK PROPER BIBLICAL DIVERSIFICATION

Divide your portion to seven, or even to eight, for you do not know what misfortune may occur on the earth. [Ecclesiastes 11:2]

Asset allocation has become an established investment strategy for those who understand the long-term nature of investing and the need to achieve an optimum level of portfolio balance and diversification in order to mitigate risk and achieve more stable returns. The core strategy involves selecting a mix of asset classes based on an investor's financial profile, investment objectives, preferences, time horizon, and risk tolerance.

The key to this strategy is the mix of asset classes that, depending on how much or how little they correlate with one another, will create a basket of counter weights that will keep the overall value of the portfolio from tipping too far in one direction. For instance, the correlation between stocks and bonds is relatively low; so when stocks perform poorly, bonds are likely to perform better. Or, during inflationary periods, precious metals are a well-known counterweight to stocks, which tend to respond poorly to inflation. A well balanced and diversified portfolio will consist of several different asset classes – stocks, bonds, precious metals, real estate, cash equivalents, etc. – all with varying levels of correlation with one another.

SEEK GOOD FINANCIAL COUNSEL

Without consultation, plans are frustrated, but with many counselors they succeed. [Proverbs 15:22]

Among the biggest mistakes investors make is to try to go it alone. With so much at stake, it's important to seek the guidance of a qualified, unbiased financial advisor. A financial advisor helps you develop your plan and discover the best investment alternatives for your particular situation.

In the realm of investment advice, value is defined by what you receive from your advisory relationship that meets or exceeds your expectations. For most people, it has much less to do with pricing or investment performance, than it has to do with the fulfillment of promises and commitments made at the outset of the relationship. But the commitments will only have value if they are based on your beliefs, values, and principles.

UNDERSTANDING RISK

A faithful man will abound with blessings, but he who makes haste to be rich will not go unpunished. [Proverbs 28:20]

Sometimes it takes people a while before they figure out that they have absolutely no control over investment performance. No one can predict the future movements of the markets or interest rates. This fixation on investment returns detracts from what investors should be focused on, and that is managing their risks. Why? Because risks are certain, and, unlike investment returns, risks can be managed. For example, we know that inflation will rise. And, we know that interest rates will rise and they will fall. You can also say with absolute certainty that the stock market will rise and it will fall.

We can't be certain of the timing or the duration, but all things economic move in cycles. The newest risk that retirees face today is also fairly certain, and that is longevity risk, or the risk of outliving one's income. When you combine the risk of longevity with the risk of inflation and the risk of declining markets, you have a compounded risk of dramatic proportions. But all of these risks can be managed and mitigated to reduce their potential impact on your financial future.

Nearly all of the mistakes made by investors can be attributed to the mismanagement of risk: underestimating or overestimating risk, not understanding risk, disregarding risk, miscalculating risk, or the failure to consider all forms of risk. Long-term investing, with the goal of accumulating sufficient capital to secure a lifetime of income in retirement, requires proactive risk management. Investors who avoid market based assets often leave themselves vulnerable to other forms of risk. Such as interest risk, inflation risk or taxation risk. Any of which can be as damaging to a retirement portfolio as market risk.

Generally, investors who focus only on the markets tend to experience a roller coaster of emotions, and their confidence is more inextricably tied to their performance. Conversely, investors who stay focused on their long-term investment strategy need only to have confidence in the strategy. If it's well conceived, with optimum diversification and is well managed through proper rebalancing and adjustments for an evolving risk tolerance, the confidence is well justified.

KEEPING IT ALL IN BIBLICAL PERSPECTIVE

Do not weary yourself to gain wealth, cease from your consideration of it. When you set your eyes on it, it is gone. For wealth certainly makes itself wings like an eagle that flies toward the heavens. [Proverbs 23:4-5]

Most people would argue that living in a digital world, with instant access to an endless stream of information, has made us smarter and more self-empowered than past generations. Investors believe that it has "leveled the playing field," enabling them to make investment decisions based on the same information once only available to the investment pros. The incessant quest for information has reached such a fever pitch that media outlets, including the cable channels, print media, and now the blogosphere, are churning out content 24/7; and that still isn't enough to satiate our ravenous appetite for information. So, it's all good? WRONG.

A much stronger argument can be made that, for people in general and investors especially, information overload not only makes it more difficult to make rational decisions, it often leads to behavior that can be harmful, if not devastating to your financial health. While there has obviously been a marked increase in the quantity of information, the quality of the information will always be in question. Where you have quantity without quality, all you really have is "noise." And for people who really should be listening for legitimate financial advice and relevant information, it can be deafening.

While it is appropriate and advisable for investors to spend time understanding and applying God's investment principles, those who spend an excessive amount of time and energy obsessing over their investments are demonstrating a lack of trust in God.

> *Trust in the* LORD *with all your heart and do not lean on your own understanding. In all your ways acknowledge Him, and He will make your paths straight.* [Proverbs 3:5-6]

Chapter Eight
LOVE OF MONEY

For the love of money is a root of all sorts of evil, and some by longing for it have wandered away from the faith and pierced themselves with many griefs. [1 Timothy 6:10]

On the flip side of God's admonishment to be content with what He provides is His contempt for those who idolize money over Him. After all, doesn't the Bible say that *"it is easier for a camel to go through the eye of a needle, than for a rich man to enter the kingdom of God?"* (Matthew 19:24) And, isn't money the *"root of all evil?"*

It is through these misinterpretations of the meaning of God's Word, that people find fault with its original premise. The Bible is long on verses about money and wealth, but nowhere does it say the two are wrong or evil. In fact, overwhelmingly, the verses of the Bible admonish us to not be lazy and work diligently so that we may prosper. Where people get it wrong is their focus on money itself, which is not the root of evil; rather it is their attitude about money about which God cautions us to be wary.

Just because you have $10 million stored away does not indicate a love of money; just as having nothing in your bank account is any indication that you don't love money. It is in your attitude and your heart that reveal your motivations. We can look at Bill Gates, one of the richest men in world, as someone who loves money because he has so much of it. Yet, his heart has led him to give away a sizable portion of it to charities. In fact, Bill Gates is leading the charge to other billionaires to give away their fortunes.

Instruct them to do good, to be rich in good works, to be generous and ready to share. [1 Timothy 6:18]

So, when we consider the scriptures of the Bible that center on prosperity and wealth, we must be especially mindful of God's true intent. He has no qualms with money, prosperity, or wealth; if they are used wisely according to His principles. It is what is in our hearts that concerns Him, and whether we are building up earthly treasures or storing up treasures in heaven.

"Do not store up for yourselves treasures on earth, where moth and rust destroy, and where thieves break in and steal. But store up for yourselves treasures in heaven, where neither moth nor rust destroys, and where thieves do not break in or steal; for where your treasure is, there your heart will be also." [Matthew 6:19-21]

HOW THE LOVE OF MONEY REVEALS ITSELF

COMPROMISE

"No one can serve two masters; for either he will hate the one and love the other, or he will be devoted to one and despise the other. You cannot serve God and wealth." [Matthew 6:24]

We are presented with opportunities (or temptations) every day to compromise where our money is concerned. It may be in the form of pocketing the extra change we receive from a cashier, slighting someone we owe, fudging the truth to make a sale, inflating the value of an item on an insurance claim, or adding a few extra miles to an expense account. On a higher scale, cheating on our taxes or filing for bankruptcy are more serious forms of compromise for which we choose the worship of money over God's Word. However we might "err" on the side of money for the sake of saving or making more, we demonstrate a willingness to compromise God's Word.

MATERIALISTIC PURSUITS

> *But seek first His kingdom and His righteousness, and all these things will be added to you. "So do not worry about tomorrow; for tomorrow will care for itself. Each day has enough trouble of its own.* [Matthew 6:33-34]

There is no sin in accumulating money or possessions, except when it overwhelms the spirit to serve. Money itself is never the problem; it is always the symptom of a problem. People often rationalize the accumulation of money and possessions as a responsible course for dealing with life's uncertainties. But God fears that the more money one accumulates without any purpose or specific plan for it, the harder it will be to overcome.

GREED

> *So are the ways of everyone who gains by violence; it takes away the life of its possessors.* [Proverbs 1:19]

All you need to do is watch a night's worth of television infomercials to realize that greed is the hot button that advertisers prey on. And their willingness to spend billions of dollars to target the greed in people is a clear sign that it lives abundantly among us. As a society, we have been conditioned to "maximize" our opportunities by earning more money, or making speculative investments; when all it does is rob us of what really matters in life. When all of our time is focused on chasing more, thinking it will bring more satisfaction, we will never find it. True satisfaction comes from God.

IS IT MONEY YOU LOVE, OR FINANCIAL FREEDOM?

> *He who loves money will not be satisfied with money, nor he who loves abundance with its income. This too is vanity.* [Ecclesiastes 5:10]

If there is one common flaw in most people's attitude about money, it is that more of it will bring financial freedom. If you know someone who has lots of money, can you say that they have financial freedom. In the pursuit of more, especially if it includes the use of debt to obtain it, no one is free financially. The stress, worry, anxiety, and pressure of chasing, investing, and keeping money enslave the mind and the spirit.

Financial freedom in the true sense is freedom from the bondage of servitude to money and debt, and finding peace and joy in the area of your finances. Peace and joy (as distinguished from "happiness" which can be fleeting) is found in believing in God's truth about wealth and riches.

> *So Jesus was saying to those Jews who had believed Him, "If you continue in My word, then you are truly disciples of Mine; and you will know the truth, and the truth will make you free."* [John 8:31-32]

Remembering that we are merely stewards of the resources on loan to us from God, we can focus more clearly on our responsibilities to apply His principles in fulfilling His plans for us. By trusting His Word that if we serve Him first, He will meet our needs, we should be able to leave our worries to Him and enjoy His peace.

And, we should remember the flip side of the Love of Money—Contentment-- if we learn how to be content with God's provisions, whatever our circumstances, He will ensure that we always have what we need.

The ultimate Financial Freedom is freedom from the Love of Money, and the ultimate antidote for it is to experience the joy of giving. It is nearly impossible to love money while giving it away in the spirit of: *"It is more blessed to give than to receive."* (Acts 20:35)

YOUR REMEDY STEPS FOR THE LOVE OF MONEY

- Make your choice. You cannot serve two masters. Put God first in your decisions about money. As cliché as it might be, asking "What would Jesus do?" is the most effective way of staying on the right track.

- Seek contentment. Don't focus on what you have or don't have; rather be content with what God has provided, knowing He will always take care of your needs.

- Do not fear money. Remember, money itself is not evil. It's your attitude about it and how you use it that can get you into trouble.

- Give freely. There's no better way to detach yourself from the materialism of money and the temptation it brings.

Chapter Nine
GETTING RICH QUICK

He who tills his land will have plenty of food, but he who follows empty pursuits will have poverty in plenty. A faithful man will abound with blessings, but he who makes haste to be rich will not go unpunished. [Proverbs 28:19-20]

Is it wrong to be rich? That is having enough money to provide for the comfort and convenience of your family and to help with needs of others, and still have more money than you will ever need? Of course, "rich" is a relative term; but in the context of your needs, it simply means that you have a surplus that can be used for any purpose beyond which you have planned and which you have shared.

God has no qualms with money, prosperity, or wealth, if it's used wisely according to His principles. He wants us to use present abundance to meet the needs of others, who in turn will use their abundance to meet our needs:

"At this present time your abundance being a supply for their need, so that their abundance also may become a supply for your need, that there may be equality; as it is written, "He who gathered much did not have too much, and he who gathered little had no lack." [2 Corinthians 8:14-15]

The problem God has with wealth is in the motives behind it and how it is obtained. Those who accumulate wealth with no other purpose than the pursuit of more, or to hoard for fear of future security, are warned to be on their guard:

> *Then He said to them, "Beware, and be on your guard against every form of greed; for not even when one has an abundance does his life consist of his possessions." And He told them a parable, saying, "The land of a rich man was very productive. And he began reasoning to himself, saying, 'What shall I do, since I have no place to store my crops?' Then he said, 'This is what I will do: I will tear down my barns and build larger ones, and there I will store all my grain and my goods. And I will say to my soul, "Soul, you have many goods laid up for many years to come; take your ease, eat, drink and be merry."' But God said to him, 'You fool! This very night your soul is required of you; and now who will own what you have prepared?' So is the man who stores up treasure for himself, and is not rich toward God."* [Luke 12:15-21]

In the Bible, the rich are admonished to guard against the temptation to trust the security that a surplus can provide. The bigger surplus one has, the greater the temptation.

> *But those who want to get rich fall into temptation and a snare and many foolish and harmful desires which plunge men into ruin and destruction. For the love of money is a root of all sorts of evil, and some by longing for it have wandered away from the faith and pierced themselves with many griefs.* [1 Timothy 6:9-10]

Now that we have a better understanding of the "spiritual" risks of getting rich quickly, let's explore the financial risks people face when they pursue fast wealth. One only has to look back a decade to get a vivid understanding of the destructive nature of the get-rich-quick mentality.

THE BIG SCAM

But those who want to get rich fall into temptation and a snare and many foolish and harmful desires which plunge men into ruin and destruction. [1 Timothy 6:9]

Thousands of people are scammed each year by dozens of get-rich-quick schemes. The most notorious scam of the modern era was guided by a former Chairman of the Board of Directors of the NASD, Bernie Madoff. You know the story. A credible and trusted investment advisor convinces his clients he can generate above market returns consistently and attracts mega worth investors. In a Ponzi fashion, he simply pays his current investors their return on investment from the monies collected from new investors. As is the case with any Ponzi scheme, the pool of new investors dried up, and he could no longer pay his current investors. Investors lost billions of dollars.

Of course, Madoff went to jail, and very few investors were able to get their investment back. It's easy to condemn Madoff for his criminal acts that were spurred by greed, but what about the hundreds of investors? What was their purpose in investing with Madoff?

THE DOT COM BOOM AND BUST

He who loves money will not be satisfied with money, nor he who loves abundance with its income. This too is vanity. [Ecclesiastes 5:10]

While it is not quite classified as a scandal or scam, it could be argued that the dot com boom and bust of the late 1990s occurred as a result of some scandalous activities on the part of investment bankers. On the way up to its peak, the dot com boom was fueled by speculation about companies that had yet to make a dollar of profit, and some had not even produced a product. Yet investment bankers were willing to create valuations and earnings forecast out of speculation that, with enough capital raised, these companies could survive and eventually thrive. Eventually the capital dried up and these companies, which essentially produced nothing, collapsed, dragging down their investors.

Again, we can fault the greed of the investment bankers and venture capitalists, but what about the millions of investors whose money inflated the bubble? What was their purpose for investing in largely unknown companies? Did they have a responsibility to understand before investing? In the pursuit of more, how much is enough?

THE LOTTO WINNER

An inheritance gained hurriedly at the beginning will not be blessed in the end. [Proverbs 20:21]

Who among us hasn't scratched a lotto ticket with visions of riches dancing in our heads? If you haven't done this, then perhaps you've harbored thoughts of a big inheritance or a windfall from some other source. The Bible warns us that too much wealth received suddenly by those ill-prepared to manage it is often frittered away. Think of the pro athletes, entertainers, and lotto winners who have squandered millions.

Quick wealth has a way of blinding us to the real value of money, often compelling us to seek more even when we don't need it. The more wealth we accumulate, the more the value of money diminishes, and that's when we completely lose sight of God's plan.

BUILDING WEALTH GOD'S WAY

The plans of the diligent lead surely to advantage, but everyone who is hasty comes surely to poverty. [Proverbs 21:5]

The Bible offers numerous contrasting visions of wealth building; it often compares those who work hard with what God has entrusted to them to those who follow worthless pursuits in the hope of getting rich quickly. It's safe to say that God prefers the former.

Wealth obtained by fraud dwindles, but the one who gathers by labor increases it. [Proverbs 13:11]

In His reasoning, the person who is suddenly wealthy has not worked hard enough to truly understand its value, and certainly doesn't have the requisite skill or motivation to manage it wisely. Conversely, those who have earned their wealth through long, diligent, and patient efforts have demonstrated the stewardship principles that will enable them to retain and grow it.

To avoid get-rich-schemes or their temptation, it's important to constantly remind yourself of what really matters in life and examine your motives for money.

But the fruit of the Spirit is love, joy, peace, patience, kindness, goodness, faithfulness, gentleness, self-control; against such things there is no law. Now those who belong to Christ Jesus have crucified the flesh with its passions and desires. [Galatians 5:22-24]

Then accept your responsibility for managing His resources wisely by investing only in what you know; not using other people's money, not making hasty decisions, diversifying your investments, and seeking good financial counsel.

It is the blessing of the Lord that makes rich, and He adds no sorrow to it. [Proverbs 10:22]

Chapter Ten
BUSINESS PRACTICES

Do you see a man skilled in his work? He will stand before kings; he will not stand before obscure men. [Proverbs 22:29]

THE HIGHER CALLING OF BUSINESS

To loosely paraphrase an overused movie line, "Profits are good, profits work." Profits – the right kind of profits – are the most effective way to create sustainable, shared economic value that can lead to true social progress that benefits the neediest among us. Admittedly, this is a rather bold claim, considering that at this very moment, business is under siege. For the last two decades, corporations have been blamed for every conceivable societal, environmental, and economic ill that has plagued the world. "Profit" has become a dirty word to describe a company's prosperity that can only be achieved at the expense of society or the environment. Today, the perceived legitimacy of their purpose and the value they create for society seem to diminish with every profit increase and every bonus paid to an executive.

Yet, at the same time, corporate social responsibility and corporate giving across all industries have increased a thousand-fold. Billions of dollars from corporate profits and employee contributions are donated each year to support social and environmental causes.

So, where's the disconnect? Why isn't business getting any credit for its contributions? Why isn't its value to society being recognized? Is business not sharing enough of its profits? Is it because business does not provide enough value? Or is it because it doesn't provide the right kind of value?

I raise these questions because I would like you to take a few moments to consider the true role of business, as contemplated by God's Word; and that what I am about to share with you is true and can be very effective.

By creating economic value in a way that also creates value for society by directly addressing its needs and challenges, for-profit businesses can not only contribute to social progress, but actually increase its profits. Does this sound too good to be true? Allow me to make the case as to why it is not.

...TEACH A MAN TO FISH, YOU FEED HIM FOR A LIFETIME

This a story of young man who, after graduating from veterinarian school, spent some time traveling through India, a country that relies heavily on working animals in all aspects of food production and commerce. A seminal moment came to him as he watched the camel drivers skillfully steer their huge, lumbering animals through the busy streets of their village lugging their wares and tools. It became clear to him that, if that animal got sick or died, the camel driver would lose his livelihood.

A sturdy male camel with twenty-five or thirty years left in its life span can fetch about $1000 these days, which few camel drivers can afford. In his position, the young man could either give the camel driver the money to buy another camel, or he could teach him how to care for it to prevent its illness and extend its utility. Even back then he knew which course would create the most economic value and affect social development, not just for the camel driver, but for his family and, ultimately, for the community.

Then he realized that if he really wanted to affect change, he couldn't rely upon other people's money to finance it – it's unreliable and, and it wouldn't be practical – he may have been idealistic but he also knew that he needed to make a living.

So when he came home, he concentrated on building a profitable business around his specialized set of skills and expertise that could be shared with less developed societies. It could produce sustainable social progress while, at the same time, enriching the lives of the people within the business. And, "enriching lives," doesn't refer to just monetary enrichment; it also refers to the enrichment of the soul – by giving employees a greater sense of purpose beyond earning a paycheck. Employees who are driven by purpose are more productive. This leads to greater profitability, which, in this business model, sustains its growth and expands its ability to create more shared value. As a result, the true economic value of profits is leveraged exponentially.

How Business Can Spread the Wealth

But you shall remember the LORD your God, for it is He who is giving you power to make wealth, that He may confirm His covenant which He swore to your fathers, as it is this day. [Deuteronomy 8:18]

Can this business model actually work? It already has. It has shown extraordinary potential to profoundly change the course of social development on a massive scale while improving the bottom lines of charitably driven companies.

What do I mean by "social development" and how is that different than corporate social responsibility or corporate charitable contributions? Social development can be described as the process of organizing human energies and activities at higher levels to achieve greater results. Social development increases the utilization of human potential. It consists of two interrelated aspects – learning and application. It occurs when society is allowed to discover better ways to fulfill its aspirations, and it is able to apply organizational mechanisms to express that knowledge in order to achieve its social and economic goals.

In other words, it's not merely about "social change," it is about changing the trajectory of society's capacity to affect its own positive economic and social progress. Businesses acting as businesses, not as charitable donors, are the most powerful force for creating the kind of economic value that can permanently change that trajectory. And, as greater number of people, including customers, employees, investors and a new generation of socially aware businesspeople, are asking business to step up and do more good.

CASE IN POINT: TOMS SHOES

An example of the power of social development through shared value that I like to use is a company called Toms, a hugely successful and highly acclaimed manufacturer of shoes. These aren't just any shoes, and, of course, this is not just your ordinary company. The founder, Blake Mycoskie, a serial entrepreneur, was traveling through Argentina when he came across entire communities of children who ran around barefoot. He discovered that these kids simply had no shoes. When he learned of the debilitating illnesses and injuries they developed from going shoeless, as well as the fact that in many of these developing societies, shoeless children are not allowed in schools, he embarked upon a mission to change all of that.

He started Toms from the ground up, with the sole purpose of covering the feet of any child who needed it. Patterned after the local footwear of Argentine farmers, Toms began to manufacture canvas shoes in different styles. For every pair of shoes sold, the company made a pair of shoes for the cause. Within the company's first year in 2006, Blake returned to Argentina with 10,000 pairs of shoes, and has since distributed hundreds of thousands more to children all around the world. The shoes that Toms provides have dramatically reduced soil transmitted disease and injuries and have enabled children to lead normal lives, attend school, and be more productive in their communities.

But the shared value created by Toms goes beyond the improved well-being of the children and their community. The company is now building manufacturing plants in some of the developing countries where shoes are needed the most, such as Argentina and Ethiopia. Toms employs hundreds of people and is accelerating the social and economic progress of those communities.

Toms may record its dollar profits on the company's bottom line, but the actual economic value of those profits and their impact on sustainable social development is incalculable.

Oh, and yes, Toms does very well. Its unique shoes, which are sold in big name stores, like Nordstrom and Whole Earth Foods, have developed a following of celebrities and famous designers, some of whom have contributed their own designs for the company. Clothing companies are lined up to partner with Toms on special clothing lines based on the shoe.

How does he make this business model work? First, he doesn't need to spend any money on marketing, which saves the company over 20 percent of their gross margin. Instead, he relies solely on the goodwill and publicity that his worldwide "shoe drops" generates. Using the power and reach of the Internet, the word on Toms spreads easily and quickly. Second, and more important for Toms, its employees are its biggest fans. People all over the world are trying to join Toms, as much to become part of the cause as they are for employment.

Blake wanted to affect social change and development. But, instead of simply starting a charity, he realized that by launching a successful, for-profit business, he could create an ever-expanding circle of economic value that would perpetually sustain both the beneficiary and the benefactor. For Blake, it was just a matter of redefining the traditional notion of "success." Success, in his terms, is not measured by profit; rather it is measured by the total economic value a dollar of profit can create by creating societal value. And, to achieve that, the company's success needs to be inextricably connected with societal improvement.

Let's return to that young man in India. After nine years of studying to become a veterinarian and a year of applying his skills in India, the young man came home to start a business. Yes, his goal was to make a profit, lots of it; because his business purpose was to create shared economic value for social development. And the more profit he could generate, the more economic value it can create. His company provides web development services and consulting to veterinary practitioners.

But, his true commitment is to create shared economic value that can improve the lives of others. In his model, for every three websites he creates, he builds a social media campaign for a developing world charitiy to raise awareness, give them a viable means of communication, and help them build a list of potential supporters.

Creating this shared economic value doesn't cost him a dime. Deploying his skills and expertise to create social media campaigns is what he does. If instead, he simply took part of his profits and sent a check, that would be a "cost," and, although it would probably serve society well, it probably would not produce any economic value beyond the amount of the check. It would not generate any real return for the business, except perhaps in good will and a clearer conscience.

On the other hand, the use of profits in the social development business model produces a sustainable, shared economic value that has the potential to grow exponentially as it directly contributes to social progress. For a business, the return on that "investment" is realized through the increased productivity and retention of employees who have a direct stake in that social progress.

SHARED ECONOMIC VALUE OR CHARITABLE CONTRIBUTIONS (WHY NOT BOTH?)

Back to the questions I raised earlier about the value of corporate social responsibility and why it isn't working. The problem that plagues even the most generous philanthropic companies is that they are trapped in an outdated approach to value creation. They continue to view value creation narrowly through the optimization of short-term financial gains. For them corporate social responsibility is a separate component that operates at the periphery of the company's core business model. It is a voluntary action they take to respond to social pressure and in many cases it is done merely to mask their shareholders' incessant appetite for profits.

Does it generate economic value? Certainly, but its value is limited by the corporate budget and the fact that it contributes very little to the company's bottom line. While it makes employees feel good about their company, the good will it creates is often only fleeting, leaving society to ask "what have you done for us lately?" Real social responsibility ought to be measured in terms of a company's ability to create shared economic value, not just social benefit.

This is not to diminish the value of corporate contributions. Lord knows we need them, and they are an important source of funding for many causes. But what I am suggesting is that a corporate social conscience and the quest for huge profits do not have to be mutually exclusive goals. In fact, when they are connected at the strategic core of a business to maximize profits, it has the potential to not only create a massive amount of shared economic value for sustainable social development; it can actually create a self-propelled mechanism for generating long-term profits.

Not all of society's ills can be solved through social development business models and shared value solutions. But shared value offers companies with the opportunity to utilize their skills, resources, and management capability to lead social progress in profound ways that even the best intentioned governmental and social sector organizations can't match. In the process, businesses can earn the respect of society again. Perhaps then, admitting that you are making a profit won't be such a bad thing.

BUSINESS SCRIPTURE FOR SUCCESS

God's plans for us most certainly include starting, managing, and growing a business to prosperity. But as with personal ambition, the Bible has plenty to say about business ambition, and the effective use of business profits for furthering His work. The same Biblical principles for managing personal finances apply equally to businesses. I find these particular verses to be especially valuable for business owners who want to steer a course guided by these sound principles.

BUSINESS BORROWING

> *"Will not all of these take up a taunt-song against him, even mockery and insinuations against him and say, 'Woe to him who increases what is not his—for how long—and makes himself rich with loans?' "Will not your creditors rise up suddenly, and those who collect from you awaken? Indeed, you will become plunder for them."* [Habakkuk 2:6-7]

Many businesses can't grow or expand without borrowed capital. While the Bible doesn't prohibit borrowing, it discourages it. Borrowing should be the last course of action, and business owners should avoid signing surety on a loan. And, long-term debt should always be a last resort.

SELF-IMPROVEMENT

All Scripture is inspired by God and profitable for teaching, for reproof, for correction, for training in righteousness. [2 Timothy 3:16]

Business owners who look for ways to improve their skills and special talents provided by God are prone to success.

INNOVATION

And do not be conformed to this world, but be transformed by the renewing of your mind, so that you may prove what the will of God is, that which is good and acceptable and perfect. [Romans 12:2]

Business success is driven by innovation, and those who strive to create new methods and technologies will lead industries.

GRATITUDE

Rejoice always; pray without ceasing; in everything give thanks; for this is God's will for you in Christ Jesus. Do not quench the Spirit. [1 Thessalonians 5:16-19]

Any business owner will tell you that things don't always go his way, and, in order to forge ahead even in the most dire circumstances, he needs to have the strength to thank God. Opportunities will follow.

PRIDE

Pride goes before destruction, and a haughty spirit before stumbling. [Proverbs 16:18]

It takes a strong ego to start and run a business, so it is not uncommon for business owners to struggle with pride. Having the courage to admit you don't have all of the answers, or to take responsibility for mistakes, will build your credibility, as well as your esteem.

OVERCOMING FEAR

For God has not given us a spirit of timidity, but of power and love and discipline. [2 Timothy 1:7]

Running a business is not for the timid, and fear has always been the enemy of entrepreneurship. God empowers us to pursue success in the face of adversity. I also like:

But Jesus, overhearing what was being spoken, said to the synagogue official, "Do not be afraid any longer, only believe." [Mark 5:36]

DISCIPLINE

All discipline for the moment seems not to be joyful, but sorrowful; yet to those who have been trained by it, afterwards it yields the peaceful fruit of righteousness. [Hebrews 12:11]

Many business failures can be attributed to a lack of discipline—financial, management, and self-discipline. If you're not an especially disciplined person, hire someone who is to keep you and the business on track.

DECISIVENESS

He who watches the wind will not sow and he who looks at the clouds will not reap. [Ecclesiastes 11:4]

Indecision is often the wrong decision in business.

COUNSEL

Where there is no guidance the people fall, but in abundance of counselors there is victory. [Proverbs 11:14]

Business owners have the vision, but they need to have several eyes focused on the business. It's important to surround yourself with advisors who have your best interests in mind. A business coach or a mentor can also provide an objective view point.

Chapter Eleven
PAYING TAXES

Honor the Lord from your wealth and from the first of all your produce; so your barns will be filled with plenty and your vats will overflow with new wine. [Proverbs 3:9-10]

For a country that was founded to avoid taxation, the United States is no shrinking violet among some of the most heavily taxed countries around the globe. With combined federal, state, local, and payroll tax rates exceeding 50 percent in some states[12] and corporate taxes second only to Japan,[13] the U.S. government's insatiable appetite for tax revenue is matched only by its unbridled propensity for spending. It currently spends twice as much as it brings in; borrows thirty-five cents of every dollar it spends; owes more than $16 trillion (tens of trillions more in unfunded liabilities); and it has been operating without a budget for more than four years.[14] The founding fathers would be hard pressed to recognize the government they formed based on Judeo-Christian principles.

---

12 Example is based on a combined tax rate comprised of 35 39.6% federal rate, 10% state income tax rate, 6.2% payroll tax. Sources: www.IRS.gov; www.ftb.ca.gov (California state tax rates)

13 KPMG International. Corporate Tax Rate Table. www.KPMG.com

14 Congressional Budget Office; Office of Management and Budget. The Budget and Economic Outlook: Fiscal Years 2013 to 2023.

The current state of fiscal dysfunction in our government has spawned a number of hardened political factions on both sides of the taxation issue. At one end of the spectrum are the Tea Party activists who favor smaller government, less spending, and a tax system overhaul. At the other end is the Occupy Wall Street crowd that favors more government, higher taxes on the rich, and more wealth redistribution. Most politicians, more intent on staying in power, are careful to avoid any association with the extremes, while doing little to address the tax and spending issues of a runaway government.

The American people seem to be somewhat ambivalent on the whole subject. Most think the government is spending too much of their money, and the vast majority feel they are taxed enough.[15] A solid majority feels the government is trying to do too much[16] while nearly half of the American public is dependent on one or more entitlements, such as food stamps and welfare.[17] Half of the working people in the U.S. pay no federal income tax, yet an equal number of people think that the rich should pay more in taxes.[18]

Suffice to say, Americans are all over the map when it comes to the government's taxing and spending. Most of us consider taxes to be a "fact of life." If we were all to be genuinely honest,

---

15 Rassmussen Reports. March 2013. 58% Worried Government Spending Won't Be Cut Enough. http://www.rasmussenreports.com/public_content/business/taxes

16 Gallup. September 2013. A majority of Americans (54%) continue to believe the government is trying to do too many things that should be left to individuals and businesses.

17 Pew Research Center. December 2012. A Bipartisan Nation of Beneficiaries. www.pewsocialtrends.org

18 Tax Policy Center. Urban Institute and Brookings Institute. Who Pays no Income Taxes? August 2013.

none of us would say that we enjoy paying them and we could all find some agreement that the government is not the best steward of our money.

Is there a case to be made that, by complying with a tax code that no one understands, and which enables the government to use our funds in ways not intended by our founding fathers, we should rise up in resistance and refuse to pay our taxes? Well, aside from it being a felony offense not to pay our taxes, the Bible also has something to say about it.

WHAT DOES THE BIBLE SAY ABOUT PAYING TAXES?

The first teaching on taxation in the Bible occurs in Genesis with what is described as the first recorded national tax on property. Pharaoh had a premonition of a seven-year famine that would strike the world. Joseph, a servant of God, devised a plan to collect 20 percent of the agricultural profits over the seven years that preceded the famine in order to provide sustenance and generate profits for Egypt when other countries came to buy their grains. Then:

> *Joseph made it a statute concerning the land of Egypt valid to this day, that Pharaoh should have the fifth; only the land of the priests did not become Pharaoh's.* [Genesis 47:26]

Later, in Leviticus, the first evidence of God's system of taxation was revealed when Levites imposed a tithe on the people of Israel.

'Thus all the tithe of the land, of the seed of the land or of the fruit of the tree, is the LORD'S; it is holy to the LORD.' [Leviticus 27:30]

If instead of grains, someone wanted to give money, they were instructed to add a fifth to the tenth, because grains were considered to be of more practical value. Although this "tax" was known as the Lord's tithe, it was also called the Levite tithe because the tenth was given to the Levites. Levites, who were the priests attending to matters of worship, also functioned as the authorities and judges of Israel.

In all, the Jews were asked to pay three taxes: a tenth for their government, a tenth for the cultivation of their national life, and three and a third for the welfare of the needy. All told, approximately 23 percent of a person's blessings were handed over to the government for the purpose of strengthening the nation. It was a government imposed system of taxation that, while not exactly beloved by the Jews, was considered fair.

These forms of institutional taxation were born out of necessity, administered from within, and served the needs of the constituents. To that extent, they seemed to work well to serve the purpose for which they were created. Nevertheless, those who avoided paying their fair share were admonished that, to do so is tantamount to robbing God:

"Will a man rob God? Yet you are robbing Me! But you say, 'How have we robbed You?' In tithes and offerings. You are cursed with a curse, for you are robbing Me, the whole nation of you!" [Malachi 3:8-9]

Most people are more familiar with the oppressive taxation of Palestine imposed by the occupying Romans. There were actually four types of taxes imposed by the Romans: a land tax, a poll tax, a tax on personal property, and a custom duties tax on exported and imported goods. In addition, the residents of Jerusalem paid a house tax. All Jews were expected to pay a half-shekel as a tithe to support the Temple in Jerusalem. By some estimates, Jews in the "highest tax brackets" paid as much as 40 percent of their earnings in taxes. To make matters worse, tax collection was a combination of brutal shakedowns by Roman officials and by profit mongering tax collectors. We thought the IRS was bad.

Most of the taxes were used to fund the Roman occupation, as well as the opulent lifestyles of the corrupt Pharisees. Funds that were not paid to the government or the temple ended up lining the pockets of the despised publicans, who were Jews contracted as tax collectors by Roman officials. Like today's bill collectors, publicans purchased the tax levies from the Romans and then turned around and collected as much as they could, pocketing the difference.

The question often raised by the oppressed Jews, not unlike the same question raised by today's Christians is: "Is it right to pay taxes to a corrupt government that misuses our money or uses it for evil purposes?" We learn a lot about God's position on taxation through the teachings of Jesus who, as a priest, was technically exempt from taxes, although the Romans didn't necessarily agree.

Jesus was tested in this regard by the Pharisees, who tried to trap Him into telling His followers not to pay their taxes, so

He would be punished by the Romans as an insurrectionist. Jesus saw through their plan and told them,

> *But Jesus perceived their malice, and said, "Why are you testing Me, you hypocrites? Show Me the coin used for the poll-tax." And they brought Him a denarius. And He said to them, "Whose likeness and inscription is this?" They said to Him, "Caesar's." Then He said to them, "Then render to Caesar the things that are Caesar's; and to God the things that are God's."* [Matthew 22:18-21]

Essentially, Jesus was telling His followers to pay their taxes and give their worship to God. However, the Jews were conflicted, because Caesar was claiming to be the son of God, and they questioned why they should pay taxes to an apostate Roman government that persecutes them. But the principle affirmed throughout the Bible is that governments, no matter how bad they are, are anointed by God as the authority to provide protection for their citizens. And that even a bad government is better than no government at all.

> *Every person is to be in subjection to the governing authorities. For there is no authority except from God, and those which exist are established by God. Therefore whoever resists authority has opposed the ordinance of God; and they who have opposed will receive condemnation upon themselves. For rulers are not a cause of fear for good behavior, but for evil. Do you want to have no fear of authority? Do what is good and you will have praise from the same; for it is a minister of God to you for good. But if you do what is evil, be afraid; for it does not bear the sword for nothing; for it is a minister of God, an avenger who brings wrath on the one who practices evil.* [Romans 13:1–4]

HOW SHOULD WE VIEW TAXATION TODAY?

If, as Paul teaches, we are bound by the word of God to submit ourselves to the government and pay our taxes, where does that leave those taxpayers who have a legitimate gripe about the way taxpayer dollars are used? Well, considering that, when Paul admonished us to pay taxes, Nero, the most evil Roman emperor in history, was the head of government, you can be sure he meant under any circumstances.

> *Therefore it is necessary to be in subjection, not only because of wrath, but also for conscience' sake. For because of this you also pay taxes, for rulers are servants of God, devoting themselves to this very thing. Render to all what is due them: tax to whom tax is due; custom to whom custom; fear to whom fear; honor to whom honor.* [Romans 13:5-7]

Therefore, we can conclude from Romans 13: 1-7 that if we don't pay taxes, we are rebelling against the authorities established by God. But, that's not to say that there are no remedies for unfair or excessive taxation. The Internal Revenue Code may be overly complex and voluminous, but it does allow for legal avoidance of taxes through a number of incentives, deductions and credits.

> *"The avoidance of taxes is the only intellectual pursuit that carries any reward."* —John Maynard Keynes

In fact, it's possible, through legitimate tax shelters and tax advantaged investments, to pay little or no taxes, depending on your sources of income. Is that rebelling against the authority and, therefore, God? No, because it is the authority that makes it possible through its tax code. Taxpayers are encouraged to avail themselves of all possible methods to reduce their taxes, but it often requires the assistance of a tax professional to navigate the complex tax code to ensure it is done legally.

As a government of the people and by the people, the tax policies are shaped largely by the electorate and who it chooses to represent them in the state and federal legislatures. The American public has already voted its preference for lower taxes, and there is a growing sentiment across party lines for a fairer tax system. While the Bible doesn't specifically prescribe a percentage or rate for a just tax, it has, by example, demonstrated that a flat tax is the fairest.

THE BIBLE'S CASE FOR THE FAIR TAX

The divine tax, otherwise known as the tithe, which literally translates into "tenth," was to be applied equally no matter the age, status, income or possessions of the individual. In fact, the Bible is explicit that we are to be impartial in our judgments when it comes to imposing a higher tax on those who "can afford it."

> *It is also not good to fine the righteous, nor to strike the noble for their uprightness.* [Proverbs 17:26]

This especially contradicts God's given purpose of civil government, which is to promote good and punish evil. When the government decides to impose higher taxes on a group of people because they have been good stewards of God's property, it punishes good habits and rewards bad ones. It seems that some in government tend to misconstrue the basic Biblical principle that it is the love of money that is the root of all evil, not money itself.

The Bible also addresses the question as to whether everyone should pay taxes. In our progressive tax system, the lowest income earners – approximately 47 percent of American taxpayers – pay no federal income tax at all.[17] In fact, many pay no tax and yet receive an earned income credit upwards of $5,000.[19] The Bible differs dramatically on this, contending that every worker should pay something in the form of income taxes:

> *This is what everyone who is numbered shall give: half a shekel according to the shekel of the sanctuary (the shekel is twenty gerahs), half a shekel as a contribution to the LORD. Everyone who is numbered, from twenty years old and over, shall give the contribution to the LORD. The rich shall not pay more and the poor shall not pay less than the half shekel, when you give the contribution to the LORD to make atonement for yourselves.* [Exodus 30:13-15]

WHAT THE BIBLE SAYS ABOUT INHERITANCE TAXES

We are constantly reminded that the only certainties in life are death and taxes. However, the government reminds us that death and taxes go hand in hand with its imposition of the death tax. The inheritance tax is considered by those on the right side of the political spectrum to be grossly unfair and harmful, especially to family farms and businesses. They believe that people shouldn't be punished for their success and should have the right to pass on the fruits of their labor. The left side of the political spectrum believes that the wealthy

19 Joint Committee on Taxation, Income Mobility and the Earned Income Tax Credit. April 2011.

should be taxed to prevent the concentration and perpetuation of wealth among the few.

A good man leaves an inheritance to his children's children, and the wealth of the sinner is stored up for the righteous. [Proverbs 13:22]

We know, based on this verse and others, that the Bible clearly encourages the transfer of a personal property to heirs. In fact, it has some very explicit instructions:

"Further, you shall speak to the sons of Israel, saying, 'If a man dies and has no son, then you shall transfer his inheritance to his daughter. If he has no daughter, then you shall give his inheritance to his brothers. If he has no brothers, then you shall give his inheritance to his father's brothers. If his father has no brothers, then you shall give his inheritance to his nearest relative in his own family, and he shall possess it; and it shall be a statutory ordinance to the sons of Israel, just as the LORD commanded Moses.'" [Numbers 27:8-11]

In terms of any government involvement in an individual's inheritance, the scriptures are also very clear:

"The prince shall not take from the people's inheritance, thrusting them out of their possession; he shall give his sons inheritance from his own possession so that My people will not be scattered, anyone from his possession." [Ezekiel 46:18]

From all indications in the Bible, God encourages us to work hard, build wealth, and enjoy it as long as it is not for the sake of wealth. For Him it all comes down to the heart.

Instruct those who are rich in this present world not to be conceited or to fix their hope on the uncertainty of riches, but on God, who richly supplies us with all things to enjoy. Instruct them to do good, to be rich in good works, to be generous and ready to share. [1 Timothy 6:17-18]

Here Paul admonishes the rich to go ahead and enjoy the fruits of their labor, but not at the expense of serving God, doing good and sharing generously. But nowhere in the Bible is it said that the government inherits any part of their wealth. One could say that the Bible offers a strictly capitalistic viewpoint on how societies should grow and prosper – free markets, low and fair taxation, the right to private property, and a government whose sole role is to protect its citizens and punish the lawless. Under God's law, the better stewards are of his property – meaning the wealthier we can become – the greater capacity we will have to do His work.

YOUR TAXATION ACTION PLAN

- Pay what is required, but not a penny more. Plan and manage your taxes in order to optimize the use of incentives, deductions, and credits that will reduce your tax burden to the extent allowable in the tax code.

- Stop loaning the government your money. If you look forward to a big refund every year, you are needlessly loaning the government your money without earning any interest. Plan your cash flow so that the least amount of taxes is withheld from your earnings.

- Make taxation a primary consideration in your investment strategy. Over a period of ten, twenty, or thirty years, taxes can take an unnecessarily significant toll on your ability to achieve your financial goals. While it's important to guard against market risk and inflation risk, taxation risk can be equally harmful. Explore the most tax efficient means to invest your money, whether you are accumulating capital or you are distributing it for income.

Chapter Twelve

WORKING AND LIFE BALANCE

For we are God's fellow workers; you are God's field, God's building. [1 Corinthians 3:9]

Despite rumors of its imminent decline, most Americans still believe that our nation is the greatest on earth because of our collective determination, our work ethic, and our unique system of government. And the rest of the world still sees it as "the land of opportunity" where anyone can achieve the American Dream through dedication and hard work. True to their Puritan heritage, Americans are working more hours than ever, although their exact motivations for doing so are based on their own economic realities of the day. For some, especially among the growing affluent, it is in the incessant pursuit of "more," while, for the shrinking middle class, it is simply to stay afloat. Ironically, no matter which end of the spectrum people find themselves, they essentially work the same long hours and make the same personal sacrifices, yet the outcomes are vastly different.

Some would say this is leading America towards a dichotomous society of the "haves" and "have nots." I suggest that the real divide is between the "workaholics," or those who see their work as their purpose in life, and the "overworked," which includes those who find themselves on an accelerating treadmill of shrinking wages chasing an elusive dream. Both are driven by pressures and incentives to work harder; and for both, their work has become the central focus of their lives. Both live to work; however, the key difference is that the former view their work as providing their personal fulfillment and sense of community, while the latter view it as a necessary means to an end.

Neither is considered particularly "bad" in the eyes of God, who, throughout the Bible, encourages us to pursue our ambitions of a good life. It was the Puritans, who came to America to practice their Christian faith without persecution, who instilled the idea that honest toil, if persevered, would lead to both mundane and spiritual rewards. Through the years, this has been translated into other forms, such as "hard work is the key to producing material wealth," and "hard work is character building and morally good."

The Puritans looked at a person's "worthiness" through their work ethic, which was often measured by what they owned—the possessions their toil enabled them to purchase. Today, having a good work ethic is what gives people credibility in society. And it was the Puritans, known for working long hours while sacrificing their quality of life, who instilled the "no pain, no gain" attitude. That conditioned us to view happiness as something that must be earned through toil, and sometimes even suffering. To this day, working is still one of the few ways we have of proving our worth and gaining possessions, and, for many people, it is at the expense of quality of life.

Recently, societal views have changed. Workaholics are no longer as esteemed for their willingness to set their personal lives aside for the sake of ambition. The rise in divorce rates, one parent households, stress-induced illnesses and deaths, and an increasing antipathy to making money for money's sake, have painted a vastly different picture of work-centric individuals. While the overworked people might garner more sympathy for their need to put work at the center of their lives, they also contribute to many of societal ills stemming from a life out of balance.

WHAT THE BIBLE MEANS ABOUT WORK/LIFE BALANCE

Interestingly, there is nothing in the Bible that distinguishes between hard work and quality of life. Consider that, in Biblical times, work life and family life were intertwined. Most people were "self-employed," working their family farm, plying their trade, or making a commerce move. Most people never left their homes to go to work, or, if they did, their families were somehow involved in their work. To a great extent, achieving a work/life balance was built into the family and economic structure of the day.

In fact, it wasn't until the Industrial Revolution that people started to venture outside their homes or their towns to earn a living, often for days or weeks at a time. People then began to lose their grip on a work/life balance. And the more prosperous the country became, the more opportunity it created for people to pursue their ambition for wealth. It was presumed that, as technology advanced and productivity increased, they would free more time for workers to spend with their families. In fact, just the opposite has happened as new technologies beget newer technologies, enabling people to find new ways of making money and squeezing more working hours out of their day.

Some might argue that little has changed since Puritan times when people toiled endlessly and sacrificed much for their gains. But Abraham Lincoln didn't see it that way. Even before the Industrial Revolution, he spoke prophetically about the unbridled pursuit of success:

> *"We have forgotten God. We have forgotten the gracious hand which preserved us in peace, and multiplied and enriched and strengthened us; and we have vainly imagined, in the deceitfulness of our hearts, that all these blessing were produced by some superior wisdom and virtue of our own. Intoxicated with unbroken success, we have become too self-sufficient to feel the necessity of redeeming and preserving grace, too proud to pray to the God that makes us."* — Abraham Lincoln, Proclamation for a National Fast Day, March 30, 1863

GOD WANTS US TO WORK HARD

Although God surely wants us to work, He doesn't want us to forget why we work, and the importance of a work/life balance.

> *Whatever you do, do your work heartily, as for the Lord rather than for men, knowing that from the Lord you will receive the reward of the inheritance. It is the Lord Christ whom you serve.* [Colossians 3:23-24]

But, in the previous verse He instructs us about the importance of maintaining a healthy family relationship:

> *Wives, be subject to your husbands, as is fitting in the Lord. Husbands, love your wives and do not be embittered against*

them. *Children, be obedient to your parents in all things, for this is well-pleasing to the Lord. Fathers, do not exasperate your children, so that they will not lose heart.* [Colossians 3:18-21]

In essence, wives and husbands must spend time in a loving relationship, and fathers are not to alienate their children. So God tells us that work and family are equally important.

...*EVEN WHEN WE DON'T LIKE THE BOSS OR OUR JOB*

In today's workplace employees often feel overworked, unappreciated, and underpaid. Many feel like slaves with no place to turn. But God has this to say to anyone enslaved to a master:

Slaves, be obedient to those who are your masters according to the flesh, with fear and trembling, in the sincerity of your heart, as to Christ; not by way of eyeservice, as men-pleasers, but as slaves of Christ, doing the will of God from the heart. With good will render service, as to the Lord, and not to men, knowing that whatever good thing each one does, this he will receive back from the Lord, whether slave or free. [Ephesians 6:5-8]

So, according to the Bible, employees are slaves? Not in the literal sense. But in the Biblical sense, there were no employees, at least in the terms we know today. Most slaves were indentured. They worked for a master under a contract that provided for food and shelter in return for a work commitment. And what God wants employees to know is that He is standing behind their employers, seeing everything we do. When we do good work, He appreciates it and He will reward us, regardless of our relationship with our employer.

WORK IS GOD'S GIFT TO US

Here is what I have seen to be good and fitting: to eat, to drink and enjoy oneself in all one's labor in which he toils under the sun during the few years of his life which God has given him; for this is his reward. Furthermore, as for every man to whom God has given riches and wealth, He has also empowered him to eat from them and to receive his reward and rejoice in his labor; this is the gift of God. [Ecclesiastes 5:18-19]

From the very beginning, God's plan is to create man to do the work of finishing His work here on earth.

Then the LORD God took the man and put him into the garden of Eden to cultivate it and keep it. [Genesis 2:15]

And, He never looks very kindly on moochers or those who chose to spend their time in other ways:

For even when we were with you, we used to give you this order: if anyone is not willing to work, then he is not to eat, either. For we hear that some among you are leading an undisciplined life, doing no work at all, but acting like busybodies. Now such persons we command and exhort in the Lord Jesus Christ to work in quiet fashion and eat their own bread. [2 Thessalonians 3:10-12]

While Solomon shows us that God wants us to enjoy the fruits of our labor, God reminds us that His provision is not unconditional. Regardless of whether we are ambitious workaholics, or struggling overworked employees, and no matter what we have to show for our work in worldly possessions, God only asks that we serve Him through our work. That includes:

SERVING OTHER PEOPLE

We are all connected by vast networks of different people and their jobs; and the products and services that are ultimately produced to serve the physical needs of others. In our work, no matter how menial, we impact the lives of many other people. Knowing that and consciously striving to do our best with that in mind is what God asks.

MEETING OUR OWN NEEDS

For even when we were with you, we used to give you this order: if anyone is not willing to work, then he is not to eat, either. [2 Thessalonians 3:10]

God is very clear that He wants us to use the talents He gave us to provide for ourselves.

MEETING OUR FAMILY'S NEEDS

But if anyone does not provide for his own, and especially for those of his household, he has denied the faith and is worse than an unbeliever. [1 Timothy 5:8]

GIVING BACK TO GOD

The one who is taught the word is to share all good things with the one who teaches him. [Galatians 6:6]

SERVING GOD

And He said to him, "YOU SHALL LOVE THE LORD YOUR GOD WITH ALL YOUR HEART, AND WITH ALL YOUR SOUL, AND WITH ALL YOUR MIND.' This is the great and foremost command-

ment. The second is like it, 'YOU SHALL LOVE YOUR NEIGHBOR AS YOURSELF.' [Matthew 22:37-39]

Through our obedience to honest work we demonstrate our obedience to God. If you connect what you do all day with what you think God wants you to be doing, as in all of the above, you will find ultimate meaning and purpose in your work.

ACHIEVING BIBLICAL BALANCE

The only other thing that God asks of us is to achieve a work/life balance that reflects His own work ethic. After all, He did create the earth in six days, and He then rested on the seventh. He created us to work: however, not to work constantly. In fact, He commanded us:

> *'Observe the sabbath day to keep it holy, as the LORD your God commanded you.'* [Deuteronomy 5:12]

Beyond that, and what He has to say about putting family relationships first, the Bible says very little specifically about work/life balance. We can look to find answers about life out of balance in what the Bible has to say about contentment.

BALANCE THROUGH CONTENTMENT

Ben Franklin was once asked about his definition of a wealthy man, and he said, "He who is contented." When asked who that is, he answered, "Nobody." Perhaps this goes with the argument that money can't buy happiness. But even for those who believe it can, happiness is only fleeting. What people really want is contentment. We know this is something that money can't buy or else there wouldn't be so many miserable, wealthy people.

While we devote a whole chapter to contentment (Chapter 5), it's covered here as it specifically relates to finding a work/life balance. At its simplest, contentment aligns what we desire with what we have. The Bible teaches us that our work cannot deliver contentment:

> *Then I looked again at vanity under the sun. There was a certain man without a dependent, having neither a son nor a brother, yet there was no end to all his labor. Indeed, his eyes were not satisfied with riches and he never asked, "And for whom am I laboring and depriving myself of pleasure?" This too is vanity and it is a grievous task.* [Ecclesiastes 4:7-8]

When people turn toward their work for contentment, searching for money, meaning, purpose or identity, their work/life balance will almost certainly tilt toward the wrong side. Instead, if you have clarity in your beliefs and values when designing your ambition for a good life, you can more clearly place it in the context of "but for the sake of what?" and distinguish it from a philosophy of "more." Money can help produce certain situations in our life, but it will never bring the fulfillment you seek.

YOUR WORK/LIFE BALANCE ACTION PLAN

- Implement your action plan for finding contentment (Chapter 5).

- Identify the ways in which your work serves God's purposes (ie: serving others, providing for myself and my family, etc.).

- Block time for balance (ie: time at the gym, time with nature, time with your family, and time for mental relaxation). Block it on your calendar so you cannot schedule something over it.

• Discover and apply your unique ability. God has given us all an incredible force, a superior ability, which is comprised of our personal talents, passions, and skills. It's in each one of us but is undiscovered and utilized by most of us. When used, it energizes us and the people around us. If you can find a way to utilize it in your work, you'll finally love what you do for a living. If not, then find a way to utilize it outside of work – volunteering. In either or both cases, it will bring much more fulfillment.

Chapter Thirteen

SUCCESS AND PROSPERITY

This book of the law shall not depart from your mouth, but you shall meditate on it day and night, so that you may be careful to do according to all that is written in it; for then you will make your way prosperous, and then you will have success. [Joshua 1:8]

Does God want us to be successful and prosperous? People of faith have been grappling with that conundrum for centuries often pitting seemingly conflicting verses of the Bible against each other in search of the truth. But it wasn't until the last few decades, a period marked by unbridled pursuit of success and prosperity, that the philosophy of "more" has drawn the close scrutiny of followers of Biblical principles. They tell us that the Bible is very clear on the matter, and that any confusion probably stems from a lack of understanding of God's intent behind those principles.

For instance, there are several well-known verses that tend to strike fear into people, making them feel as if they should run from money or success. I've often heard the following verse quoted by those who are quick to criticize successful or prosperous Christians for their hypocrisy:

"For it is easier for a camel to go through the eye of a needle than for a rich man to enter the kingdom of God." [Luke 18:25]

But, as numerous Biblical passages teach us, the amount of success or prosperity a person achieves is irrelevant. God wants us to live abundantly. The issue becomes muddled when our love of money or our ambition begins to rise above our love for God. Here Jesus is telling us that, in the quest for success or money, it is easy for a person to become attached to material things and thoughts of riches that have no place in heaven. But wealth alone does not disqualify someone from entering the gates of heaven; rather, it is people's attitude about money and success, and their priorities that God questions. It's when people equate success purely with financial wealth and material things that they begin to veer off course.

GOD PRAISES SUCCESS

Throughout the Bible, diligence, hard work and success are praised and said to be worthy of God's blessings and promises of greater abundance. Jesus framed the virtues of success best in this Parable of the Talents:

"For it is just like a man about to go on a journey, who called his own slaves and entrusted his possessions to them. To one he gave five talents, to another, two, and to another, one, each according to his own ability; and he went on his journey. Immediately the one who had received the five talents went and traded with them, and gained five more talents. In the same manner the one who had received the two talents gained two more. But he who received the one talent went away, and dug a hole in the ground and hid his master's money.

"*Now after a long time the master of those slaves came and settled accounts with them. The one who had received the five talents came up and brought five more talents, saying, 'Master, you entrusted five talents to me. See, I have gained five more talents.' His master said to him, 'Well done, good and faithful slave. You were faithful with a few things, I will put you in charge of many things; enter into the joy of your master.'*

"*Also the one who had received the two talents came up and said, 'Master, you entrusted two talents to me. See, I have gained two more talents.' His master said to him, 'Well done, good and faithful slave. You were faithful with a few things, I will put you in charge of many things; enter into the joy of your master.'*

"*And the one also who had received the one talent came up and said, 'Master, I knew you to be a hard man, reaping where you did not sow and gathering where you scattered no seed. And I was afraid, and went away and hid your talent in the ground. See, you have what is yours.'*

"*But his master answered and said to him, 'You wicked, lazy slave, you knew that I reap where I did not sow and gather where I scattered no seed. Then you ought to have put my money in the bank, and on my arrival I would have received my money back with interest. Therefore take away the talent from him, and give it to the one who has the ten talents.'*

"*For to everyone who has, more shall be given, and he will have an abundance; but from the one who does not have, even what he does have shall be taken away. Throw out the worthless slave into the outer darkness; in that place there will be weeping and gnashing of teeth.*" [Matthew 25:14-30]

Not only does Jesus praise the success of the productive stewards, He has equal disdain for the one who was unwilling to take risks and try for success. In casting the "wicked and lazy slave" out for his failure, Jesus was not frustrated with his lack of production; rather he was angry that the steward did not use his God-given ability to even try. As the passage states, the master gave to each of them according to their ability; so, even though he was given only one talent, the master felt he had some ability, or he wouldn't have given him the one.

Do not neglect the spiritual gift within you, which was bestowed on you through prophetic utterance with the laying on of hands by the presbytery. [1 Timothy 4:14]

We are all given talents from God, and He expects us to use them to create abundance, whether it is in the form of spiritual growth or temporal things. All that matters to God is that we put Him first:

But seek first His kingdom and His righteousness, and all these things will be added to you. [Matthew 6:33]

Our priorities must first be in order, and then we can keep the proper perspective of success as God intended. I think the late Zig Ziglar, a devout Christian and the world's most famous success coach, framed it perfectly when he said:

"Success means doing the best we can with what we have. Success is the doing, not the getting—in the trying, not the triumph. Success is a personal standard—reaching for the highest that is in us—becoming all that we can be. If we do our best, we are a success. Success is the maximum utilization of the ability that you have."

In our own ambition for a good life, success should be measured not in terms of wealth, fame, status, or power; rather, in how we use it to better our lives, as well as the lives of those around us.

> *Do nothing from selfishness or empty conceit, but with humility of mind regard one another as more important than yourselves.* [Philippians 2:3]

Or, as Ziglar said, "*You can get everything in life you want if you will just help other people get what they want.*"

HOW SHOULD WE FEEL ABOUT PROSPERITY?

Success is often equated with prosperity, because having one usually implies having the other. Yet, some people see ambiguities in the Bible as it relates to prosperity and the possession of temporal goods. For instance, Matthew admonishes us to:

> "*Do not store up for yourselves treasures on earth, where moth and rust destroy, and where thieves break in and steal. But seek first His kingdom and His righteousness, and all these things will be added to you.*" [Matthew 6:19,33]

Some might read this to mean, in effect, that God isn't interested in whether I am successful or prosperous, just that I put Him first. We are told throughout the Bible that God will provide us with what we need, and that we should be content with what He provides.

But, we are also told that, if we put Him first and pay our tithes, He will:

> "*Open for you the windows of heaven and pour out for you a blessing until it overflows.*" [Malachi 3:10]

So, which is it? Perhaps God wants us to be conflicted so we are forced to search more deeply to understand His intent; because, to know God is to know that He has a purpose for everything.

GOD REJOICES IN OUR PROSPERITY

Throughout the Bible we are told that God has pleasure in the prosperity of His servants:

> *Let them shout for joy and rejoice, who favor my vindication; and let them say continually, "The LORD be magnified, who delights in the prosperity of His servant."* [Psalm 35:27]

But, He constantly reminds us that prosperity does not come from our own power; rather it is given to us by His power:

> *But you shall remember the LORD your God, for it is He who is giving you power to make wealth, that He may confirm His covenant which He swore to your fathers, as it is this day.* [Deuteronomy 8:18]

All that He asks is that we trust in Him and live our lives with purpose:

> *Delight yourself in the LORD; and He will give you the desires of your heart.* [Psalms 37:4]

It is clear that God wants us to be prosperous, and we know He has a purpose in doing so. But should that mean we forgo our own enjoyment of our prosperity, and *lay not up for [ourselves] treasures upon earth...*? In Ecclesiastes, Solomon offers a greater context for what God wants from us:

> *Moreover he hath not seen the sun, nor known any thing: this hath more rest than the other. Yea, though he lives a thousand*

years twice told, yet hath he seen no good: do not all go to one place? All the labor of man is for his mouth, and yet the appetite is not filled. [Ecclesiastes 6:5-7]

Through Solomon, a highly successful and prosperous servant of God, Ecclesiastes explores the vanity of the present by pointing out that great possessions mean nothing of themselves. Through Solomon's search for the greatest good in life, he learns that true success and accomplishment cannot be measured by possessions. Possessions give no assurance of happiness or peace. To find true happiness, we must go much deeper for the answer to life's great purpose.

For Solomon, who believed that wealth without happiness is fruitless and that family without appreciation is unfulfilling, it was essential that he find the practical morality in his prosperity. He did so by realizing that he couldn't see into the future, so all of the benefits of his labor should be obtained in the present. The future holds nothing but unfulfilled desires, so it is better to find contentment in the present by enjoying the fruits of our labor.

His reasoning was that a man could give himself to the pursuit of wealth; or he could give himself to the pursuit of wisdom. Only a fool seeks neither. Yet they all end up in the same place. The Wisdom of Solomon is in striking the right balance by moderating our pursuit of wealth while laying up treasures in heaven.

THE PURPOSE OF SUCCESS AND PROSPERITY

But the one who did not know it, and committed deeds worthy of a flogging, will receive but few. From everyone who has been given much, much will be required; and to whom they entrusted much, of him they will ask all the more. [Luke 12:48]

God has it all worked out. When we understand that our success and prosperity is a blessing from God, it is easier to understand our purpose in achieving it; and through that, live a much more fulfilling life. We are all given some unique ability that God expects us to fully utilize in creating a good life for ourselves; and then to expand our circle of good fortune to help others. And, because God continues to bless those who do good, the circle can continue to grow.

YOUR SUCCESS AND PROSPERITY ACTION PLAN

- Count your blessings. Take stock of what God has given you and seek to find contentment in it.

- Define success in your terms. What is the outcome you are seeking – financially, physically, and/or spiritually?

- Review your goals and ambitions. What's their stated purpose? What will achieving them bring you both in temporal and spiritual gains? Does their purpose include a benefit for God?

- List three ways you will use your success and prosperity to benefit others in the coming year, and then hold yourself accountable.

Chapter Fourteen
STEWARDSHIP SCRIPTURES

Clearly, the Bible has a lot to say about possessions and finances; so much so that it devotes more than 2,000 verses, more than 15 percent of its content, to the topic. That's more than it devotes to any other single topic, including Heaven, Hell, faith, or prayer! If we didn't know better, we might conclude that God's intent is to micromanage our financial management. Actually, that is the last thing He wants to do. That's why He gave us free will to make our own choices. But He did so with an important caveat: that we follow His guidance and adhere to Biblical principles.

> *The mind of man plans his way, but the LORD directs his steps.*
> [Proverbs 16:9]

THE STEWARDSHIP COVENANT

The Biblical principles covered extensively in this book have at their core a single underlying precept based on a covenant made between God and His children:

> *But seek first His kingdom and His righteousness, and all these things will be added to you.* [Matthew 6:33]

With that, God assures us that if we live our lives based on His priorities, He will provide what we need. All that He asks is that we find contentment in what He provides. However, He also wants to see us prosper and is willing to '...*open for you the windows of heaven and pour out for you a blessing until it overflows.*' [Malachi 3:10]

But for the sake of what? Remember, God established a covenant which means that His promise is conditional upon a promise we make to Him:

> *And God is able to make all grace abound to you, so that always having all sufficiency in everything, you may have an abundance for every good deed.* [2 Corinthians 9:8]

To bring more clarity and a proper perspective to this arrangement, God adds one more all- important caveat:

> *"Do not store up for yourselves treasures on earth, where moth and rust destroy, and where thieves break in and steal. But seek first His kingdom and His righteousness, and all these things will be added to you."* [Matthew 6:19,33]

MANAGING WHAT IS ENTRUSTED TO US

The Bible teaches us that, since we came into this world with nothing, we will ultimately leave this world with nothing. Everything we possess is given to us by God and therefore, it all belongs to God. So, in the short time we have on earth, we are in essence, stewards of his property, which we must manage for the benefit of everyone, especially those in need. And the better we do as His stewards, the more treasures we will lay up in Heaven for ourselves.

The Bible essentially is a guide for stewardship that lays down the principles, and, in many instances, the actual instructions we are to follow in the management of His possessions. At its simplest, we are directed to manage our money, not in our own self-interest, but in a way that is in line with His priorities and His wishes for His property. In doing so, we will store more treasures in Heaven and God will bless us with prosperity.

As stewards of God's property—and that entails all that we have been given, including our time, talents, and treasure—we must ask ourselves at the end of each day, "Was I faithful with what God has entrusted to me?" In anticipation of that question, we are compelled to conduct ourselves and make financial decisions in ways that we know will please God:

> *As each one has received a special gift, employ it in serving one another as good stewards of the manifold grace of God.* [1 Peter 4:10]

THE MEASURE OF A GOOD STEWARD

Just as employees are held accountable by their manager and promoted or demoted for their performance, we are held accountable by God for the way we manage His resources. As stewards, we may not be subjected to annual evaluations, but God has His own way of providing feedback, which is manifested in how much is entrusted to us.

> *"He who is faithful in a very little thing is faithful also in much; and he who is unrighteous in a very little thing is unrighteous also in much."* [Luke 16:10]

While God praises and heaps blessings on those who are faithful in their stewardship, He holds nothing but scorn for those who squander His possessions. There is no better illustration of this than the Parable of the Talents. A full reading is available in Chapter 7– Investing, so I'll just summarize here:

> *A very wealthy man about to leave on a long trip decides to divide his talents (money) among his servants. It was no small amount of money, either. In the day, a talent was worth 6,000 days of work. He gave each servant an amount of talents he felt was appropriate for their abilities. When he returned, he asked the three servants what they had done with money. The servant with the most talents said he doubled his money, as did the servant with the second most amount of talents. The servant with the least amount of talents told his master that he didn't gain any because he buried them so he wouldn't lose any. After praising the successful servants he took the third servant's talents and gave them to the others. He then cast the "wicked and lazy" servant out.*

It doesn't take a theologian to decipher this parable. Jesus is reminding us that God has given each of us talents and abilities to be used, not to be squandered. We will be rewarded with additional blessings for our diligence and punished for our laziness. The talents were not given to the servants; they were simply loaned to them, the same way in which our own talents and possession are on loan from God.

In telling the Parable of the Talents, Jesus was making another very important point. The three servants were each given a different amount of money according to their abilities. In life, we are each given different gifts, and some people start out with more than others. But the number of talents we have, or what we start out with, is irrelevant. It's what we do with our gifts that matters. And it doesn't matter how much more success one has with his gifts versus another with his. While both of the successful servants doubled their money, the one who started with less actually had more success; but that didn't matter to the wealthy man. They were both equally praised. God sees it the same way. As long as you use the gifts given to you, that is all that matters.

God gives all of us the opportunity prosper in a way that will allow us to live our own vision of a good life. And we each have our own vision of what constitutes a good life; God's purpose for giving us the ability to achieve it is the same for everyone – to do good on His behalf.

From everyone who has been given much, much will be required; and to whom they entrusted much, of him they will ask all the more. [Luke 12:48]

Ultimately, we will all be judged on how well we managed His resources during our time on earth:

For we must all appear before the judgment seat of Christ, so that each one may be recompensed for his deeds in the body, according to what he has done, whether good or bad. [2 Corinthians 5:10]

GOOD STEWARDSHIP OFTEN REQUIRES TRAINING

Even though we are all born with God given talents, most people aren't inherently blessed with the ability to manage all of the disciplines required of us, such as financial management. That so many people are deep in debt is testimony to the fact that humans are prone to succumbing to bad habits and the cultural influences of the day.

Successful money management also requires patience and discipline, which are not instinctive traits for many people. The combination of traits and knowledge that is required for successful money management is not easy to acquire, but is essential in order to achieve the financial freedom necessary to be a good steward.

Successful money management starts with an understanding of what is required of you; and that you take some initial steps to align your finances with the key principles of finance, which is the purpose of this book. But it takes diligence and commitment to develop the traits and knowledge to see your financial plan through to fruition. Certainly, books and workshops are a great way to build a foundation of knowledge.

Your best resource, however, is to work with a competent, objective, and independent financial advisor, especially one who shares your values and beliefs. Not only will your education be targeted to your specific needs, a good financial advisor is also a good coach who helps you to develop the discipline and patience to stay on course.

YOUR STEWARDSHIP ACTION PLAN

Develop a plan to expand your stewardship capacity.

First, focus on those things you do well and do more of them. Make a list of a unique ability, special talent, valuable skill, or an aspect of your life that, if you could find a way to expand them, would expand your circle of value to include others.

1. _____
2. _____
3. _____

For each, describe how you can increase your level of commitment to develop it for the benefit of others.

1. _____
2. _____
3. _____

Next, identify three aspects of your life that you want to improve. By doing so, allowing you to give more of yourself to others (ie: time management, community involvement, honing skills or knowledge).

1. _____
2. _____
3. _____

Then write down ONE practical step you can take to grow in each area.

1. _____
2. _____
3. _____

Develop an action plan and timeline for each and track your progress daily.

Chapter Fifteen

FINDING FINANCIAL COUNSEL

Without consultation, plans are frustrated, but with many counselors they succeed. [Proverbs 15:22]

In Chapter 6—Planning, we debunked the notion that to plan our financial future is a demonstration of our distrust in God. Quite the contrary, God wants us to plan and be prepared so we can be better stewards. This is why He laid down clear Biblical financial principles for us to follow.

Clearly the financial world has grown much more complex in the centuries since the Bible was written. Our financial lives are increasingly influenced by forces beyond our control. Such as: the global economy, government taxation, regulations and fiscal policies, and media-driven cultural pressures. It's no wonder that the vast majority of Americans are frozen in confusion and fear. This is why they procrastinate or fail completely to do the necessary planning.

Today, the way financial planning needs to be done is very daunting to most people. Done right, it entails assessing, analyzing, prioritizing, and implementing all of the pieces of the financial puzzle so they fit together in a coordinated, comprehensive plan.

Consider all of the pieces that are a part of the financial puzzle:

Financial Management

- Cash reserve levels
- Cash reserve strategies
- Debt management

- Giving
- Expected large out-flows and inflows
- Lines of Credit

- Net worth
- Cash flow management

Protection Planning

- Disability options
- Long-term care
- Umbrella liability
- Alternate additional coverage strategies

- Medical health
- Property casualty
- Policy status
- Deductibles vs. cash reserves

- Policy loans
- Beneficiary designation
- Life insurance
- Special needs situations

Savings and Investments

- Investment objectives
- Retirement savings
- Understanding risk/ return
- College savings

- Asset allocation strategy
- Diversification
- Monitoring investment performance

- Stocks, bonds, commodities, real estate, ETFs, mutual funds, precious metals

Tax Planning

- Tax reduction
- Tax deferral
- Tax avoidance
- Future taxes due

- Witholding tax
- Tax diversification
- Qualified investments
- Non-qualified investments

- Filing status
- Tax on distributions
- Business ownership
- Non-traditional ownership

Estate Planning

- Estate balancing
- Capital transfer
- Asset ownership
- Estate liquidity

- Trusts
- Wills
- Guardianship
- Trust funding

- Special needs funding
- Succession planning
- Estate settlement
- Charitable giving

IT'S NOT THE PLAN; IT'S THE EXECUTION

In our practice, we frequently meet with prospective clients who are not satisfied with their existing advisor because their plan is not working. Yet, when we review the financial plan developed by their advisor, we find that it contains many of the elements of a sound plan that can actually mirror our own, with many of same principles and practices we follow. But it didn't work, so the client wants a new advisor, with a new strategy.

Our real work begins. It starts with an educational process to help our new clients understand that it's generally not the advisor's financial plan that matters most in achieving their financial objectives – it's their behavior that matters. If a financial plan and investment strategy call for patience, discipline, and faith in the future, and they insist on breaking from the strategy (ie: fleeing the market in times of panic or buying into a raging market with the rest of the herd), it simply won't work.

The key to successful long-term planning and investing is to have faith in the future. The patience is to see it unfold as it is meant to happen, and the discipline to stay the course. Here's what the Bible says about Faith in the Future, Patience, and Discipline, and their importance in financial planning:

FAITH IN THE FUTURE

"So do not worry about tomorrow; for tomorrow will care for itself. Each day has enough trouble of its own." [Matthew 6:34]

Good stewards view the future optimistically, because, to do otherwise would ignore the Word of God. When facing financial difficulties, we are told:

And my God will supply all your needs according to His riches in glory in Christ Jesus. [Philippians 4:19]

Your faith in the future can help you keep the events of the day in perspective, no matter how cataclysmic. Local, national, and global events can be consequential to our lives in the moment. However, their impact on our financial lives may be diminished over a 20 to 30 year time horizon.

When we have faith in the future, we don't know exactly how things will turn out; we just know that they will turn out all right. So we can plan and invest accordingly.

PATIENCE

> *For in hope we have been saved, but hope that is seen is not hope; for who hopes for what he already sees? But if we hope for what we do not see, with perseverance we wait eagerly for it.* [Romans 8:24-25]

In financial planning and investing, exercising patience is less about doing the right thing and more about having the presence of mind to avoid doing the wrong things. Successful investors are able to withstand the pain of missing some of the upside in the market, or riding out a market decline, in order to minimize the typical and often devastating mistakes that unsuccessful investors make. Patient investors don't know when everything is going to turn out all right; they just know that it will eventually. So, they invest accordingly.

DISCIPLINE

> *All discipline for the moment seems not to be joyful, but sorrowful; yet to those who have been trained by it, afterwards it yields the peaceful fruit of righteousness.* [Hebrews 12:11]

Whereas patience represents the presence of mind to avoid doing the wrong thing at the wrong time, discipline is the exercise of the mind to do the right thing by staying the course. The ability to exercise self-discipline in the face of challenging circumstances doesn't come naturally for most people. But those who are able to do so are better able to inoculate themselves from the emotional tirades of the media and the herd.

Because the exercise of discipline is a conscious action, it needs to be reinforced by certain beliefs that the action will lead to the best possible results. Without faith in the future or the patience to persevere, there is essentially no spine to support the very challenging and often painful act of exercising discipline.

To exercise discipline means ignoring the fads, trends, noise, gurus, herds, and even pronouncements of the next big thing. Because what appears to be working right now is not nearly as important as what has always worked. Discipline is the adherence to those things that have always worked most reliably.

WHY YOU NEED A FINANCIAL COACH

> *The way of a fool is right in his own eyes, but a wise man is he who listens to counsel.* [Proverbs 12:15]

With human nature being what it is, most people, especially the males of the species, are not genetically coded with the attributes of patience and discipline; and recent events have turned a lot of people into cynics regarding the future. We are emotional creatures, and it's emotions that tend to guide our decisions, especially regarding financial planning and investing. And that is what leads to our breaking strategy.

The best analogy I can use with my new clients is my recent attempt to get back into fitness. To ensure that I had a plan and I would be doing everything correctly according to my objectives, I hired a trainer. We customized an exercise and nutrition regimen and began training twice a week. After two months, I felt as if I knew exactly what to do so I fired my trainer. I had the plan and I knew the regimen, so why pay him more money?

After one more trip to the gym, I stopped going. Something always came up or I had some excuse for not getting to the gym. But the biggest obstacle was my mind, which constantly convinced me that I was too tired or too busy to take time to work out. I now realize why we pay trainers. It's not to give us the plan or the regimen, but to avoid the behavioral traps that causes us to lose focus and abandon discipline. It's the trainer who holds us accountable and pushes us to achieve a level of performance beyond our current experience.

Executing a financial plan is no different than exercising. It requires a goal, a plan, a strategy, and implementation to be successful. Many good financial advisors have the ability to develop sound financial plans and investment strategies. The one who breaks strategy is not the advisor; it's usually the client.

Developing the financial plan is actually the easy part. The hard part, as financial advisors earning our pay, is to keep our clients focused on the target while coaching them to maintain patience, discipline, and faith in the future. Essentially, our primary job is to keep our clients from falling into the typical behavioral traps that can severely hurt their chances of achieving their long-term goals.

A good financial advisor is also a "life coach" who helps you to navigate all aspects of your financial life and put all of the pieces of your financial puzzle together. He/she has access to the expertise and resources to help you manage your finances holistically; taking into account your needs and objectives in the areas of taxes, insurance, debt management, estate planning, and lifestyle planning.

FINDING THE RIGHT FINANCIAL ADVISOR

The challenge for investors is finding the right financial advisor. The sheer number of financial professionals who claim to be "financial advisors" (nearly 300,000 at last count) makes this a daunting task at best.[20] The task is made easier if you know what to look for, but that requires an acute sense of what you want exactly from an advisory relationship.

In the realm of financial advice, value is defined by what you receive from your advisory relationship that meets or exceeds your expectations. For most clients, it has much less to do with pricing or investment performance, than it has to do with the fulfillment of promises and commitments made at the outset of the relationship. But the commitments will only have value if they are based on your own values, beliefs, and stated needs and expectations. So, unless you are able to clearly articulate what you expect, any commitments will hold little, if any, value.

THE BIBLE AS A GUIDE FOR FINDING GOOD FINANCIAL COUNSEL

SEEK WISE, UNBIASED COUNSEL

"No one can serve two masters; for either he will hate the one and love the other, or he will be devoted to one and despise the other. You cannot serve God and wealth." [Matthew 6:24]

---

20 Investment News. Adviser numbers will continue to slide: Cerulli. InvestmentNews.com. May 2013

Because financial advisors are not all the same, individuals are left with the task of discerning which one they should work with. Just as an employer conducts a thorough background check and interviews a prospective employee, it's also important to thoroughly assess your financial advisor.

SEEK THE COUNSEL OF THOSE LIKE YOU

> *How blessed is the man who does not walk in the counsel of the wicked, nor stand in the path of sinners, nor sit in the seat of scoffers!* [Psalm 1:1]

If you are to live your financial life according to Biblical financial principles, it's important to find a like-minded financial advisor who shares your values, beliefs, and principles. Does that mean you should only work with a devout Christian advisor? Not necessarily. You need competence and experience as well. You could come across any number of financial advisors who profess to be Christians, but whose lifestyle is not the least bit Christ-like. And you could also find those advisors who are very good Christians, but they lack the wisdom of Biblical principles of finances. You should interview several prospective financial advisors in order to find the one that "clicks" in all respects.

SEEK A TEAM APPROACH TO FINANCIAL COUNSEL

> *Without consultation, plans are frustrated, but with many counselors they succeed.* [Proverbs 15:22]

The body of knowledge and competencies required to develop and implement a comprehensive financial plan, integrating multiple disciplines that address both personal and business needs, is as extensive as any that any individual must be able to acquire in his or her own professional field. In fact, it is far beyond the capacity of any one professional advisor, which is why the most qualified and client-centric advisors insist on a "team approach" to developing and implementing a comprehensive financial plan.

SEEK COMPETENT FINANCIAL ADVISORS

> *A wise man will hear and increase in learning, and a man of understanding will acquire wise counsel.* [Proverbs 1:5]

While it's important to work with a financial advisor who shares your values and beliefs, it is equally important that you find one with the competence, experience, and breadth of knowledge required for such a critical position. Look for financial advisors with at least five years of experience, professional designations (CFP, ChFC), a clean background, community involvement, and a client profile that matches yours.

The best source for finding prospective advisors is through people you trust – your friends, colleagues, and family members—who can provide a strong testament to the value they received.

YOUR GUIDE FOR FINDING FINANCIAL COUNSEL

- Make a list of the values and beliefs most important to you and incorporate them into a personal philosophy statement of how you want to live your life. You don't need to show this to anyone, but it will provide you with a compass to determine if a financial advisor is on your track.

- Ask for at least five referrals from trusted friends and family, and find out what they perceive to be the true value of their relationship with their advisor.

- Select only the ones who are independent (not affiliated with a brokerage or insurance firm), credentialed (CFP, ChFC), and experienced (5 plus years).

- Conduct a quick background check:

  ☑ Check their website. Study their mission statement, philosophy, services offered, and their bios. If they don't have one it may be a red flag.

  ☑ Do a broker-check. Go to www.brokercheck.finra.org for their dossier which includes licensing, employment history, any customer disputes or disciplinary actions.

  ☑ Google them. A Google search could uncover more information, such as awards, community involvement, and/or articles written.

- Get ready to interview. Select at least two or three advisors to interview. Make a list of questions. These are some very effective questions I've been asked by prospective clients:

  ☑ How is your firm compensated on transactions and will that be disclosed to me?

  ☑ Will you disclose to me any potential conflict of interest, including your relationships with any party that could interfere with your ability to put my interest first in all matters?

  ☑ How do you measure client performance?

  ☑ Who will be working directly with me? If not you, when will I be able to interview the others?

☑ What is your typical client profile, and how does mine match up with theirs?

☑ How many clients do you have, and what can I expect in the amount of attention you can give me?

- Ask Your "Gut" questions:

  ☑ Has the advisor made you feel comfortable in your interactions? How would your mother react to his mannerisms and temperament? Seriously!

  ☑ Is this a person who you can truly entrust with your financial legacy?

  ☑ Does the advisor explain things to educate you or to simply demonstrate how much he knows?

  ☑ Do you feel that you will gain something of value (knowledge, insight, positive approach, etc.) from a relationship with this advisor that you wouldn't obtain from another?

  ☑ Don't go it alone. Pray for God's guidance in one of the most important decisions you'll ever make.

REVIEW OF PERSONAL FINANCE SCRIPTURES

INTRODUCTION

FINANCIAL PRINCIPLES STEEPED IN WISDOM

He who loves money will not be satisfied with money, nor he who loves abundance with its income. This too is vanity. [Ecclesiastes 5:10]

"Therefore everyone who hears these words of Mine and acts on them, may be compared to a wise man who built his house on the rock. And the rain fell, and the floods came, and the winds blew and slammed against that house; and yet it did not fall, for it had been founded on the rock. Everyone who hears these words of Mine and does not act on them, will be like a foolish man who built his house on the sand. The rain fell, and the floods came, and the winds blew and slammed against that house; and it fell—and great was its fall." [Matthew 7:24-27]

PRINCIPLE #1: LIVE WITHIN YOUR MEANS

There is precious treasure and oil in the dwelling of the wise, but a foolish man swallows it up. [Proverbs 21:20]

Principle #2: Live Debt-Free

The rich rules over the poor, and the borrower becomes the lender's slave. [Proverbs 22:7]

PRINCIPLE #3: BUILD RESERVES

Go to the ant, O sluggard, observe her ways and be wise, which, having no chief, officer or ruler, prepares her food in the summer and gathers her provision in the harvest. [Proverbs 6:6-8]

PRINCIPLE #4: ESTABLISH LONG-TERM GOALS

The mind of man plans his way, but the LORD directs his steps. [Proverbs 16:9]

PRINCIPLE #5: SEEK FINANCIAL COUNSEL

He who walks with wise men will be wise, but the companion of fools will suffer harm. [Proverbs 13:20]

IF YOU CAN'T TAKE IT WITH YOU— DOES IT REALLY BELONG TO YOU?

For we have brought nothing into the world, so we cannot take anything out of it either. [1 Timothy 6:7]

'For I know the plans that I have for you,' declares the LORD, 'plans for welfare and not for calamity to give you a future and a hope.' [Jeremiah 29:11]

His master said to him, 'Well done, good and faithful slave. You were faithful with a few things, I will put you in charge of many things; enter into the joy of your master.' [Matthew 25:23]

THE WISDOM TO SAVE US FROM OURSELVES

By wisdom a house is built, and by understanding it is established; and by knowledge the rooms are filled with all precious and pleasant riches. [Proverbs 24:3-4]

CHAPTER 1—BUDGETING

THE VIRTUE OF DILIGENCE

Know well the condition of your flocks, and pay attention to your herds. [Proverbs 27:23]

For riches are not forever, nor does a crown endure to all generations. [Proverbs 27:24]

BE PREPARED

Go to the ant, O sluggard, observe her ways and be wise, which, having no chief, officer or ruler, prepares her food in the summer and gathers her provision in the harvest. [Proverbs 6:6-8]

ESTABLISH A SPENDING PLAN

On the first day of every week each one of you is to put aside and save, as he may prosper, so that no collections be made when I come. [1 Corinthians 16:2]

AVOID TEMPTATION

Like a city that is broken into and without walls is a man who has no control over his spirit. [Proverbs 25:28]

PLAN AHEAD

For which one of you, when he wants to build a tower, does not first sit down and calculate the cost to see if he has enough to com-

plete it? Otherwise, when he has laid a foundation and is not able to finish, all who observe it begin to ridicule him, saying, 'This man began to build and was not able to finish.' [Luke 14:28-30]

CHAPTER 2—DEBT

The rich rules over the poor, and the borrower becomes the lender's slave. [Proverbs 22:7]

SHOULD I USE CREDIT CARDS?

The prudent sees the evil and hides himself, but the naive go on, and are punished for it. [Proverbs 22:3]

Do not be among those who give pledges, among those who become guarantors for debts. If you have nothing with which to pay, why should he take your bed from under you? [Proverbs 22:26-27]

YOUR GOOD NAME IS MORE VALUABLE THAN MONEY

A good name is to be more desired than great wealth, favor is better than silver and gold. [Proverbs 22:1]

BECOME KNOWLEDGEABLE ABOUT DEBT

The naive believes everything, but the sensible man considers his steps. [Proverbs 14:15]

GETTING OUT OF DEBT

Then she came and told the man of God. And he said, "Go, sell the oil and pay your debt, and you and your sons can live on the rest." [2 Kings 4:7]

And do not be conformed to this world, but be transformed by the renewing of your mind, so that you may prove what the will of God is, that which is good and acceptable and perfect. [Romans 12:2]

SUMMARY

The Lord will open for you His good storehouse, the heavens, to give rain to your land in its season and to bless all of the work of your hand; and you shall lend to many nations, but you shall not borrow. [Deuteronomy 28:12]

CHAPTER 3—SAVING

There is precious treasure and oil in the dwelling of the wise, but a foolish man swallows it up. [Proverbs 21:20]

SAVING FOR THE FUTURE

Go to the ant, O sluggard, observe her ways and be wise, which, having no chief, officer or ruler, prepares her food in the summer and gathers her provision in the harvest. [Proverbs 6:6-8]

ALL WE REALLY HAVE IS TIME

He who watches the wind will not sow and he who looks at the clouds will not reap. [Ecclesiastes 11:4]

SAVING FOR A PURPOSE

But God said to him, 'You fool! This very night your soul is required of you; and now who will own what you have prepared?' So is the man who stores up treasure for himself, and is not rich toward God." [Luke 12:20-21]

SAVING FROM THE HEART

So then, while we have opportunity, let us do good to all people, and especially to those who are of the household of the faith. [Galatians 6:10]

"Do not store up for yourselves treasures on earth, where moth and rust destroy, and where thieves break in and steal. But store up for yourselves treasures in heaven, where neither moth nor rust destroys, and where thieves do not break in or steal; for where your treasure is, there your heart will be also." [Matthew 6:19-21]

CHAPTER 4—GIVING

In everything I showed you that by working hard in this manner you must help the weak and remember the words of the Lord Jesus, that He Himself said, 'It is more blessed to give than to receive.'" [Acts 20:35]

And He sat down opposite the treasury, and began observing how the people were putting money into the treasury; and many rich people were putting in large sums. A poor widow came and put in two small copper coins, which amount to a cent. Calling His disciples to Him, He said to them, "Truly I say to you, this poor widow put in more than all the contributors to the treasury; for they all put in out of their surplus, but she, out of her poverty, put in all she owned, all she had to live on." [Mark 12:41-45]

Each one must do just as he has purposed in his heart, not grudgingly or under compulsion, for God loves a cheerful giver. [2 Corinthians 9:7]

THE PRINCIPLE OF TITHING

"Bring the whole tithe into the storehouse, so that there may be food in My house, and test Me now in this," says the LORD of hosts,

"if I will not open for you the windows of heaven and pour out for you a blessing until it overflows." [Malachi 3:10]

"Woe to you, scribes and Pharisees, hypocrites! For you tithe mint and dill and cummin, and have neglected the weightier provisions of the law: justice and mercy and faithfulness; but these are the things you should have done without neglecting the others." [Matthew 23:23]

THE NEW COVENANT OF GIVING

"put aside and save, as he may prosper." [1 Corinthians 16:2]

"Each one must do just as he has purposed in his heart, not grudgingly or under compulsion, for God loves a cheerful giver." [2 Corinthians 9:7]

"prove through the earnestness of others the sincerity of your love also." [2 Corinthians 8:8]

Now this I say, he who sows sparingly will also reap sparingly, and he who sows bountifully will also reap bountifully. Each one must do just as he has purposed in his heart, not grudgingly or under compulsion, for God loves a cheerful giver. [2 Corinthians 9:6-7]

The generous man will be prosperous, and he who waters will himself be watered. [Proverbs 11:25]

Therefore if you have not been faithful in the use of unrighteous wealth, who will entrust the true riches to you? [Luke 16:11]

Give, and it will be given to you. They will pour into your lap a good measure—pressed down, shaken together, and running over. For by your standard of measure it will be measured to you in return." [Luke 6:38]

"I never would have been able to tithe the first million dollars I ever made if I had not tithed my first salary, which was $1.50 per week." – John D. Rockefeller

WE HAVE RESPONSIBILITIES

From everyone who has been given much, much will be required; and to whom they entrusted much, of him they will ask all the more. [Luke 12:48]

Even so faith, if it has no works, is dead, being by itself. [James 2:17]

His master said to him, 'Well done, good and faithful slave. You were faithful with a few things, I will put you in charge of many things; enter into the joy of your master.' [Matthew 25:23]

CHAPTER 5—CONTENTMENT

The Lord is my shepherd, I shall not want. [Psalm 23:1]

LEARNING CONTENTMENT

For we have brought nothing into the world, so we cannot take anything out of it either. If we have food and covering, with these we shall be content. But those who want to get rich fall into temptation and a snare and many foolish and harmful desires which plunge men into ruin and destruction. [1 Timothy 6:7-9]

But godliness actually is a means of great gain when accompanied by contentment. [1 Timothy 6:6]

Then He said to them, "Beware, and be on your guard against every form of greed; for not even when one has an abundance does his life consist of his possessions." [Luke 12:15]

CONFIDENCE AND CONTENTMENT GO HAND-IN-HAND

Not that I speak from want, for I have learned to be content in whatever circumstances I am. I know how to get along with humble means, and I also know how to live in prosperity; in any and every circumstance I have learned the secret of being filled and going hungry, both of having abundance and suffering need. I can do all things through Him who strengthens me. [Philippians 4:11-13]

Make sure that your character is free from the love of money, being content with what you have; for He Himself has said, "I WILL NEVER DESERT YOU, NOR WILL I EVER FORSAKE YOU." [Hebrews 13:5]

YOUR ACTION STEPS FOR LEARNING CONTENTMENT

And the peace of God, which surpasses all comprehension, will guard your hearts and your minds in Christ Jesus. [Philippians 4:7]

CHAPTER 6—PLANNING

WHAT THE BIBLE SAYS ABOUT PLANNING

But seek first His kingdom and His righteousness, and all these things will be added to you. "So do not worry about tomorrow; for tomorrow will care for itself. Each day has enough trouble of its own. [Matthew 6:33-34]

Go to the ant, O sluggard, observe her ways and be wise, which, having no chief, officer or ruler, prepares her food in the summer and gathers her provision in the harvest. [Proverbs 6:6-8]

The plans of the diligent lead surely to advantage, but everyone who is hasty comes surely to poverty. [Proverbs 21:5]

GOD WANTS US TO PLAN AND PREPARE

The mind of man plans his way, but the Lord directs his steps. [Proverbs 16:9]

SET PRIORITIES

Prepare your work outside and make it ready for yourself in the field; afterwards, then, build your house. [Proverbs 24:27]

REDUCE YOUR RISK

The prudent sees the evil and hides himself, but the naive go on, and are punished for it. [Proverbs 22:3]

COUNT ON CHANGE

Come now, you who say, "Today or tomorrow we will go to such and such a city, and spend a year there and engage in business and make a profit." Yet you do not know what your life will be like tomorrow. You are just a vapor that appears for a little while and then vanishes away. [James 4:13-14]

KNOW HOW MUCH YOUR GOALS WILL COST

For which one of you, when he wants to build a tower, does not first sit down and calculate the cost to see if he has enough to complete it? [Luke 14:28]

TAKE ACTION

In all labor there is profit, but mere talk leads only to poverty. [Proverbs 14:23]

A Word about Insurance

But if anyone does not provide for his own, and especially for those of his household, he has denied the faith and is worse than an unbeliever. [1 Timothy 5:8]

CHAPTER 7—INVESTING

The plans of the diligent lead surely to advantage, but everyone who is hasty comes surely to poverty. [Proverbs 21:5]

So He said, "A nobleman went to a distant country to receive a kingdom for himself, and then return. And he called ten of his slaves, and gave them ten minas and said to them, 'Do business with this until I come back.' But his citizens hated him and sent a delegation after him, saying, 'We do not want this man to reign over us.' When he returned, after receiving the kingdom, he ordered that these slaves, to whom he had given the money, be called to him so that he might know what business they had done. The first appeared, saying, Master, your mina has made ten minas more.' And he said to him, 'Well done, good slave, because you have been faithful in a very little thing, you are to be in authority over ten cities.' The second came, saying, 'Your mina, master, has made five minas.' And he said to him also, 'And you are to be over five cities.' Another came, saying, 'Master, here is your mina, which I kept put away in a handkerchief; for I was afraid of you, because you are an exacting man; you take up what you did not lay down and reap what you did not sow.' He said to him, 'By your own words I will judge you, you worthless slave. Did you know that I am an exacting man, taking up what I did not lay down and reaping what I did not sow? Then why did you not put my money in the bank, and having come, I would have collected it with interest?' Then he said to the bystanders, 'Take the mina

*away from him and give it to the one who has the ten minas.'
And they said to him, 'Master, he has ten minas already.' I tell you
that to everyone who has, more shall be given, but from the one
who does not have, even what he does have shall be taken away."*
[Luke 19:12-26]

All the ways of a man are clean in his own sight, but the LORD
weighs the motives. [Proverbs 16:2]

*But seek first His kingdom and His righteousness, and all these
things will be added to you.* [Matthew 6:33]

INVEST CONDITIONALLY

*Prepare your work outside and make it ready for yourself in the
field; afterwards, then, build your house.* [Proverbs 24:27]

APPLYING GOD'S PRINCIPLES

*Also it is not good for a person to be without knowledge, and he
who hurries his footsteps errs.* [Proverbs 19:2]

INVEST ONLY IN WHAT YOU UNDERSTAND

*The mind of the prudent acquires knowledge, and the ear of the
wise seeks knowledge.* [Proverbs 18:15]

DO NOT OVER-LEVERAGE YOUR INVESTMENTS

*The rich rules over the poor, and the borrower becomes the lender's
slave.* [Proverbs 22:7]

DON'T MAKE HASTY DECISIONS

*The plans of the diligent lead surely to advantage, but everyone
who is hasty comes surely to poverty.* [Proverbs 21:5]

SEEK PROPER BIBLICAL DIVERSIFICATION

Divide your portion to seven, or even to eight, for you do not know what misfortune may occur on the earth. [Ecclesiastes 11:2]

SEEK GOOD FINANCIAL COUNSEL

Without consultation, plans are frustrated, but with many counselors they succeed. [Proverbs 15:22]

UNDERSTANDING RISK

A faithful man will abound with blessings, but he who makes haste to be rich will not go unpunished. [Proverbs 28:20]

KEEPING IT ALL IN BIBLICAL PERSPECTIVE

Do not weary yourself to gain wealth, cease from your consideration of it. When you set your eyes on it, it is gone. For wealth certainly makes itself wings like an eagle that flies toward the heavens. [Proverbs 23:4-5]

Trust in the LORD with all your heart and do not lean on your own understanding. In all your ways acknowledge Him, and He will make your paths straight. [Proverbs 3:5-6]

CHAPTER 8—LOVE OF MONEY

For the love of money is a root of all sorts of evil, and some by longing for it have wandered away from the faith and pierced themselves with many griefs. [1 Timothy 6:10]

It is easier for a camel to go through the eye of a needle, than for a rich man to enter the kingdom of God. [Matthew 19:24]

Instruct them to do good, to be rich in good works, to be generous and ready to share. [1 Timothy 6:18]

"Do not store up for yourselves treasures on earth, where moth and rust destroy, and where thieves break in and steal. But store up for yourselves treasures in heaven, where neither moth nor rust destroys, and where thieves do not break in or steal; for where your treasure is, there your heart will be also. " [Matthew 6:19-21]

COMPROMISE

"No one can serve two masters; for either he will hate the one and love the other, or he will be devoted to one and despise the other. You cannot serve God and wealth." [Matthew 6:24]

MATERIALISTIC PURSUITS

But seek first His kingdom and His righteousness, and all these things will be added to you. "So do not worry about tomorrow; for tomorrow will care for itself. Each day has enough trouble of its own. [Matthew 6:33-34]

GREED

So are the ways of everyone who gains by violence; it takes away the life of its possessors. [Proverbs 1:19]

IS IT MONEY YOU LOVE, OR FINANCIAL FREEDOM?

He who loves money will not be satisfied with money, nor he who loves abundance with its income. This too is vanity. [Ecclesiastes 5:10]

So Jesus was saying to those Jews who had believed Him, "If you continue in My word, then you are truly disciples of Mine; and you will know the truth, and the truth will make you free." [John 8:31-32]

"It is more blessed to give than to receive." [Acts 20:35]

CHAPTER 9—GETTING RICH QUICK

He who tills his land will have plenty of food, but he who follows empty pursuits will have poverty in plenty. A faithful man will abound with blessings, but he who makes haste to be rich will not go unpunished. [Proverbs 28:19-20]

"At this present time your abundance being a supply for their need, so that their abundance also may become a supply for your need, that there may be equality; as it is written, "HE WHO gathered MUCH DID NOT HAVE TOO MUCH, AND HE WHO gathered LITTLE HAD NO LACK." [2 Corinthians 8:14-15]

Then He said to them, "Beware, and be on your guard against every form of greed; for not even when one has an abundance does his life consist of his possessions." And He told them a parable, saying, "The land of a rich man was very productive. And he began reasoning to himself, saying, 'What shall I do, since I have no place to store my crops?' Then he said, 'This is what I will do: I will tear down my barns and build larger ones, and there I will store all my grain and my goods. And I will say to my soul, "Soul, you have many goods laid up for many years to come; take your ease, eat, drink and be merry."' But God said to him, 'You fool! This very night your soul is required of you; and now who will own what you have prepared?' So is the man who stores up treasure for himself, and is not rich toward God." [Luke 12:15-21]

But those who want to get rich fall into temptation and a snare and many foolish and harmful desires which plunge men into ruin and destruction. For the love of money is a root of all sorts of evil, and some by longing for it have wandered away from the faith and pierced themselves with many griefs. [1 Timothy 6:9-10]

THE BIG SCAM

But those who want to get rich fall into temptation and a snare and many foolish and harmful desires which plunge men into ruin and destruction. [1 Timothy 6:9]

THE DOT COM BOOM AND BUST

He who loves money will not be satisfied with money, nor he who loves abundance with its income. This too is vanity. [Ecclesiastes 5:10]

THE LOTTO WINNER

An inheritance gained hurriedly at the beginning will not be blessed in the end. [Proverbs 20:21]

BUILDING WEALTH GOD'S WAY

The plans of the diligent lead surely to advantage, but everyone who is hasty comes surely to poverty. [Proverbs 21:5]

Wealth obtained by fraud dwindles, but the one who gathers by labor increases it. [Proverbs 13:11]

But the fruit of the Spirit is love, joy, peace, patience, kindness, goodness, faithfulness, gentleness, self-control; against such things there is no law. Now those who belong to Christ Jesus have crucified the flesh with its passions and desires. [Galatians 5:22-24]

It is the blessing of the Lord that makes rich, and He adds no sorrow to it. [Proverbs 10:22]

CHAPTER 10 —BUSINESS PRACTICES

Do you see a man skilled in his work? He will stand before kings; he will not stand before obscure men. [Proverbs 22:29]

HOW BUSINESS CAN SPREAD THE WEALTH

But you shall remember the LORD your God, for it is He who is giving you power to make wealth, that He may confirm His covenant which He swore to your fathers, as it is this day. [Deuteronomy 8:18]

BUSINESS BORROWING

"Will not all of these take up a taunt-song against him, even mockery and insinuations against him and say, 'Woe to him who increases what is not his—for how long—and makes himself rich with loans?' "Will not your creditors rise up suddenly, and those who collect from you awaken? Indeed, you will become plunder for them." [Habakkuk 2:6-7]

SELF-IMPROVEMENT

All Scripture is inspired by God and profitable for teaching, for reproof, for correction, for training in righteousness. [2 Timothy 3:16]

INNOVATION

And do not be conformed to this world, but be transformed by the renewing of your mind, so that you may prove what the will of God is, that which is good and acceptable and perfect. [Romans 12:2]

GRATITUDE

Rejoice always; pray without ceasing; in everything give thanks; for this is God's will for you in Christ Jesus. Do not quench the Spirit. [1 Thessalonians 5:16-19]

PRIDE

Pride goes before destruction, and a haughty spirit before stumbling. [Proverbs 16:18]

OVERCOMING FEAR

For God has not given us a spirit of timidity, but of power and love and discipline. [2 Timothy 1:7]

But Jesus, overhearing what was being spoken, said to the synagogue official, "Do not be afraid any longer, only believe." [Mark 5:36]

DISCIPLINE

All discipline for the moment seems not to be joyful, but sorrowful; yet to those who have been trained by it, afterwards it yields the peaceful fruit of righteousness. [Hebrews 12:11]

DECISIVENESS

He who watches the wind will not sow and he who looks at the clouds will not reap. [Ecclesiastes 11:4]

COUNSEL

Without the guidance of good leaders a nation falls. But many good advisers can save it. [Proverbs 11:14]

CHAPTER 11—PAYING TAXES

Honor the Lord from your wealth and from the first of all your produce; so your barns will be filled with plenty and your vats will overflow with new wine. [Proverbs 3:9-10]

WHAT DOES THE BIBLE SAY ABOUT PAYING TAXES?

Joseph made it a statute concerning the land of Egypt valid to this day, that Pharaoh should have the fifth; only the land of the priests did not become Pharaoh's. [Genesis 47:26]

'Thus all the tithe of the land, of the seed of the land or of the fruit of the tree, is the LORD'S; it is holy to the LORD.' [Leviticus 27:30]

"Will a man rob God? Yet you are robbing Me! But you say, 'How have we robbed You?' In tithes and offerings. You are cursed with a curse, for you are robbing Me, the whole nation of you!" [Malachi 3:8-9]

But Jesus perceived their malice, and said, "Why are you testing Me, you hypocrites? Show Me the coin used for the poll-tax." And they brought Him a denarius. And He said to them, "Whose likeness and inscription is this?" They said to Him, "Caesar's." Then He said to them, "Then render to Caesar the things that are Caesar's; and to God the things that are God's." [Matthew 22:18-21]

Every person is to be in subjection to the governing authorities. For there is no authority except from God, and those which exist are established by God. Therefore whoever resists authority has opposed the ordinance of God; and they who have opposed will receive condemnation upon themselves. For rulers are not a cause of fear for good behavior, but for evil. Do you want to have no fear of authority? Do what is good and you will have praise from the same; for it is a minister of God to you for good. But if you do what is evil, be afraid; for it does not bear the sword for nothing; for it is a minister of God, an avenger who brings wrath on the one who practices evil. [Romans 13:1–4]

HOW SHOULD WE VIEW TAXATION TODAY?

Therefore it is necessary to be in subjection, not only because of wrath, but also for conscience' sake. For because of this you also pay taxes, for rulers are servants of God, devoting themselves to this very thing. Render to all what is due them: tax to whom tax is due; custom to whom custom; fear to whom fear; honor to whom honor. [Romans 13:5-7]

"The avoidance of taxes is the only intellectual pursuit that carries any reward." —John Maynard Keynes

THE BIBLE'S CASE FOR THE FAIR TAX

It is also not good to fine the righteous, nor to strike the noble for their uprightness. [Proverbs 17:26]

This is what everyone who is numbered shall give: half a shekel according to the shekel of the sanctuary (the shekel is twenty gerahs), half a shekel as a contribution to the LORD. Everyone who is numbered, from twenty years old and over, shall give the contribution to the LORD. The rich shall not pay more and the poor shall not pay less than the half shekel, when you give the contribution to the LORD to make atonement for yourselves. [Exodus 30:13-15]

WHAT THE BIBLE SAYS ABOUT INHERITANCE TAXES

A good man leaves an inheritance to his children's children, and the wealth of the sinner is stored up for the righteous. [Proverbs 13:22]

"Further, you shall speak to the sons of Israel, saying, 'If a man dies and has no son, then you shall transfer his inheritance to his daughter. If he has no daughter, then you shall give his inheritance to his brothers. If he has no brothers, then you shall give his inheritance to his father's brothers. If his father has no brothers, then you shall give his inheritance to his nearest relative in his own family, and he shall possess it; and it shall be a statutory ordinance to the sons of Israel, just as the LORD commanded Moses.'" [Numbers 27:8-11]

"The prince shall not take from the people's inheritance, thrusting them out of their possession; he shall give his sons inheritance from his own possession so that My people will not be scattered, anyone from his possession." [Ezekiel 46:18]

Instruct those who are rich in this present world not to be conceited or to fix their hope on the uncertainty of riches, but on God, who richly supplies us with all things to enjoy. Instruct them to do good, to be rich in good works, to be generous and ready to share. [1 Timothy 6:17-18]

CHAPTER 12—WORKING AND LIFE BALANCE

For we are God's fellow workers; you are God's field, God's building. [1 Corinthians 3:9]

WHAT THE BIBLE MEANS ABOUT WORK/LIFE BALANCE

"We have forgotten God. We have forgotten the gracious hand which preserved us in peace, and multiplied and enriched and strengthened us; and we have vainly imagined, in the deceitfulness of our hearts, that all these blessing were produced by some superior wisdom and virtue of our own. Intoxicated with unbroken success, we have become too self-sufficient to feel the necessity of redeeming and preserving grace, too proud to pray to the God that makes us." —Abraham Lincoln, Proclamation for a National Fast Day, March 30, 1863

GOD WANTS US TO WORK HARD

Whatever you do, do your work heartily, as for the Lord rather than for men, knowing that from the Lord you will receive the reward of the inheritance. It is the Lord Christ whom you serve. [Colossians 3:23-24]

Wives, be subject to your husbands, as is fitting in the Lord. Husbands, love your wives and do not be embittered against them. Children, be obedient to your parents in all things, for this is well-pleasing to the Lord. Fathers, do not exasperate your children, so that they will not lose heart. [Colossians 3:18-21]

...Even when we don't like the boss or our job

Slaves, be obedient to those who are your masters according to the flesh, with fear and trembling, in the sincerity of your heart, as to Christ; not by way of eyeservice, as men-pleasers, but as slaves of Christ, doing the will of God from the heart. With good will render service, as to the Lord, and not to men, knowing that whatever good thing each one does, this he will receive back from the Lord, whether slave or free. [Ephesians 6:5-8]

Work is God's Gift to Us

Here is what I have seen to be good and fitting: to eat, to drink and enjoy oneself in all one's labor in which he toils under the sun during the few years of his life which God has given him; for this is his reward. Furthermore, as for every man to whom God has given riches and wealth, He has also empowered him to eat from them and to receive his reward and rejoice in his labor; this is the gift of God. [Ecclesiastes 5:18-19]

Then the Lord God took the man and put him into the garden of Eden to cultivate it and keep it. [Genesis 2:15]

For even when we were with you, we used to give you this order: if anyone is not willing to work, then he is not to eat, either. For we hear that some among you are leading an undisciplined life, doing no work at all, but acting like busybodies. Now such persons we command and exhort in the Lord Jesus Christ to work in quiet fashion and eat their own bread. [2 Thessalonians 3:10-12]

MEETING OUR OWN NEEDS

For even when we were with you, we used to give you this order: if anyone is not willing to work, then he is not to eat, either. [2 Thessalonians 3:10]

MEETING OUR FAMILY'S NEEDS

But if anyone does not provide for his own, and especially for those of his household, he has denied the faith and is worse than an unbeliever. [1 Timothy 5:8]

GIVING BACK TO GOD

The one who is taught the word is to share all good things with the one who teaches him. [Galatians 6:6]

SERVING GOD

And He said to him, "YOU SHALL LOVE THE LORD YOUR GOD WITH ALL YOUR HEART, AND WITH ALL YOUR SOUL, AND WITH ALL YOUR MIND.' This is the great and foremost commandment. The second is like it, 'YOU SHALL LOVE YOUR NEIGHBOR AS YOURSELF.' [Matthew 22:37-39]

ACHIEVING BIBLICAL BALANCE

'Observe the sabbath day to keep it holy, as the LORD your God commanded you.' [Deuteronomy 5:12]

BALANCE THROUGH CONTENTMENT

Then I looked again at vanity under the sun. There was a certain man without a dependent, having neither a son nor a brother, yet there was no end to all his labor. Indeed, his eyes were not satisfied with riches and he never asked, "And for whom am I laboring and depriving myself of pleasure?" This too is vanity and it is a grievous task. [Ecclesiastes 4:7-8]

CHAPTER 13—SUCCESS AND PROSPERITY

This book of the law shall not depart from your mouth, but you shall meditate on it day and night, so that you may be careful to do according to all that is written in it; for then you will make your way prosperous, and then you will have success. [Joshua 1:8]

"For it is easier for a camel to go through the eye of a needle than for a rich man to enter the kingdom of God." [Luke 18:25]

GOD PRAISES SUCCESS

"For it is just like a man about to go on a journey, who called his own slaves and entrusted his possessions to them. To one he gave five talents, to another, two, and to another, one, each according to his own ability; and he went on his journey. Immediately the one who had received the five talents went and traded with them, and gained five more talents. In the same manner the one who had received the two talents gained two more. But he who received the one talent went away, and dug a hole in the ground and hid his master's money.

"Now after a long time the master of those slaves came and settled accounts with them. The one who had received the five talents came up and brought five more talents, saying, 'Master, you en-

trusted five talents to me. See, I have gained five more talents.' His master said to him, 'Well done, good and faithful slave. You were faithful with a few things, I will put you in charge of many things; enter into the joy of your master.'

"Also the one who had received the two talents came up and said, 'Master, you entrusted two talents to me. See, I have gained two more talents.' His master said to him, 'Well done, good and faithful slave. You were faithful with a few things, I will put you in charge of many things; enter into the joy of your master.'

"And the one also who had received the one talent came up and said, 'Master, I knew you to be a hard man, reaping where you did not sow and gathering where you scattered no seed. And I was afraid, and went away and hid your talent in the ground. See, you have what is yours.'

"But his master answered and said to him, 'You wicked, lazy slave, you knew that I reap where I did not sow and gather where I scattered no seed. Then you ought to have put my money in the bank, and on my arrival I would have received my money back with interest. Therefore take away the talent from him, and give it to the one who has the ten talents.'

"For to everyone who has, more shall be given, and he will have an abundance; but from the one who does not have, even what he does have shall be taken away. Throw out the worthless slave into the outer darkness; in that place there will be weeping and gnashing of teeth." [Matthew 25:14-30]

Do not neglect the spiritual gift within you, which was bestowed on you through prophetic utterance with the laying on of hands by the presbytery. [1 Timothy 4:14]

But seek first His kingdom and His righteousness, and all these things will be added to you. [Matthew 6:33]

"Success means doing the best we can with what we have. Success is the doing, not the getting—in the trying, not the triumph. Success is a personal standard—reaching for the highest that is in us—becoming all that we can be. If we do our best, we are a success. Success is the maximum utilization of the ability that you have." —Zig Ziglar

Do nothing from selfishness or empty conceit, but with humility of mind regard one another as more important than yourselves. [Philippians 2:3]

"You can get everything in life you want if you will just help other people get what they want." —Zig Ziglar

HOW SHOULD WE FEEL ABOUT PROSPERITY?

"Do not store up for yourselves treasures on earth, where moth and rust destroy, and where thieves break in and steal. But seek first His kingdom and His righteousness, and all these things will be added to you." [Matthew 6:19,33]

"Open for you the windows of heaven and pour out for you a blessing until it overflows." [Malachi 3:10]

GOD REJOICES IN OUR PROSPERITY

Let them shout for joy and rejoice, who favor my vindication; and let them say continually, "The LORD be magnified, who delights in the prosperity of His servant." [Psalm 35:27]

But you shall remember the LORD your God, for it is He who is giving you power to make wealth, that He may confirm

His covenant which He swore to your fathers, as it is this day. [Deuteronomy 8:18]

Delight yourself in the LORD; and He will give you the desires of your heart. [Psalms 37:4]

It never sees the sun and it never knows anything; it is better off than he. Even if the other man lives a thousand years twice and does not enjoy good things—do not all go to one place?" All a man's labor is for his mouth and yet the appetite is not satisfied. [Ecclesiastes 6:5-7]

THE PURPOSE OF SUCCESS AND PROSPERITY

But the one who did not know it, and committed deeds worthy of a flogging, will receive but few. From everyone who has been given much, much will be required; and to whom they entrusted much, of him they will ask all the more. [Luke 12:48]

CHAPTER 14—STEWARDSHIP SCRIPTURES

The mind of man plans his way, but the Lord directs his steps. [Proverbs 16:9]

THE STEWARDSHIP COVENANT

But seek first His kingdom and His righteousness, and all these things will be added to you. [Matthew 6:33]

'Open for you the windows of heaven and pour out for you a blessing until it overflows.' [Malachi 3:10]

And God is able to make all grace abound to you, so that always having all sufficiency in everything, you may have an abundance for every good deed. [2 Corinthians 9:8]

"Do not store up for yourselves treasures on earth, where moth and rust destroy, and where thieves break in and steal. But seek first His kingdom and His righteousness, and all these things will be added to you." [Matthew 6:19,33]

MANAGING WHAT IS ENTRUSTED TO US

As each one has received a special gift, employ it in serving one another as good stewards of the manifold grace of God. [1 Peter 4:10]

THE MEASURE OF A GOOD STEWARD

"He who is faithful in a very little thing is faithful also in much; and he who is unrighteous in a very little thing is unrighteous also in much." [Luke 16:10]

From everyone who has been given much, much will be required; and to whom they entrusted much, of him they will ask all the more. [Luke 12:48]

For we must all appear before the judgment seat of Christ, so that each one may be recompensed for his deeds in the body, according to what he has done, whether good or bad. [2 Corinthians 5:10]

CHAPTER 15—FINDING FINANCIAL COUNSEL

Without consultation, plans are frustrated, but with many counselors they succeed. [Proverbs 15:22]

FAITH IN THE FUTURE

"So do not worry about tomorrow; for tomorrow will care for itself. Each day has enough trouble of its own." [Matthew 6:34]

And my God will supply all your needs according to His riches in glory in Christ Jesus. [Philippians 4:19]

PATIENCE

For in hope we have been saved, but hope that is seen is not hope; for who hopes for what he already sees? But if we hope for what we do not see, with perseverance we wait eagerly for it. [Romans 8:24-25]

DISCIPLINE

All discipline for the moment seems not to be joyful, but sorrowful; yet to those who have been trained by it, afterwards it yields the peaceful fruit of righteousness. [Hebrews 12:11]

WHY YOU NEED A FINANCIAL COACH

The way of a fool is right in his own eyes, but a wise man is he who listens to counsel. [Proverbs 12:15]

SEEK WISE, UNBIASED COUNSEL

No one can serve two masters; for either he will hate the one and love the other, or he will be devoted to one and despise the other... [Matthew 6:24]

SEEK THE COUNSEL OF THOSE LIKE YOU

How blessed is the man who does not walk in the counsel of the wicked, nor stand in the path of sinners, nor sit in the seat of scoffers! [Psalm 1:1]

SEEK A TEAM APPROACH TO FINANCIAL COUNSEL

Without consultation, plans are frustrated, but with many counselors they succeed. [Proverbs 15:22]

SEEK COMPETENT FINANCIAL ADVISORS

A wise man will hear and increase in learning, and a man of understanding will acquire wise counsel. [Proverbs 1:5]

Sources

[1] The 2012 National Financial Capability Study conducted by the FINRA Education Foundation http://www.usfinancialcapability.org.

[2] US Department of Labor, Bureau of Labor Statistics. Employment Situation Summary. July 2013. (11.2 million unemployed as of July 2013, and 8.5 million involuntary part-time workers).

[3&4] Federal Reserve G-19 Consumer Credit Report. January 2013. (As of January 2013, Americans held $850.9 billion in credit card debt or $6,920 per household; $1.944 trillion in school, auto, furniture loans, or $15,800 per household.)

[5] American Consumer Credit Counseling (ACCC). ConsumerCredit.com, Debt Payoff Calculator ($15,000 of debt at an assumed rate of 12 percent and a minimum monthly payment of $15).

[6] Employee Benefit Research Institute. 2013 Retirement Confidence Survey.

[7] 2010 Wells Fargo Retirement Fitness Survey. www.WellsFargo.com

[8] U.S. Department of Commerce: Bureau of Economic Analysis. 2013 http://research.stlouisfed.org

[9] Barna Group. April 2012. The Economy Continues to Squeeze American's Charitable Giving. www.barna.org

[10] Social Security Administration. Life Expectancy for Retirement and Survivor Benefits. www.socialsecurity.gov

[11] 2013 Milliman Medical Index. www.Milliman.com

[12] Example is based on a combined tax rate comprised of 35 39.6% federal rate, 10% state income tax rate, 6.2% payroll tax. Sources: www.IRS.gov; www.ftb.ca.gov (California state tax rates)

[13] KPMG International. Corporate Tax Rate Table. www.KPMG.com

[14] Congressional Budget Office; Office of Management and Budget. The Budget and Economic Outlook: Fiscal Years 2013 to 2023.

[15] Rassmussen Reports. March 2013. 58% Worried Government Spending Won't Be Cut Enough. http://www.rasmussenreports.com/public_content/business/taxes

[16] Gallup. September 2013. A majority of Americans (54%) continue to believe the government is trying to do too many things that should be left to individuals and businesses.

[17] Pew Research Center. December 2012. A Bipartisan Nation of Beneficiaries. www.pewsocialtrends.org

[18] Tax Policy Center. Urban Institute and Brookings Institute. Who Pays no Income Taxes? August 2013.

[19] Joint Committee on Taxation, Income Mobility and the Earned Income Tax Credit. April 2011.

[20] Investment News. Adviser numbers will continue to slide: Cerulli. InvestmentNews.com. May 2013